Diagrammatic representation of the basic features of coral polyps and skeletons.

Computer design by Jan Balon, after Dr. Elizabeth M. Wood.

A GUIDE TO THE SELECTION, CARE & BREEDING OF CORALS FOR THE MINI-REEF AQUARIUM

BY DR. HERBERT R. AXELROD

© 1997 BY DR. HERBERT R. AXELROD

Distributed in the UNITED STATES to the Pet Trade by T.F.H. Publications, Inc., One T.F.H. Plaza, Neptune City, NJ 07753; distributed in the UNITED STATES to the Bookstore and Library Trade by National Book Network, Inc. 4720 Boston Way, Lanham MD 20706; in CANADA to the Pet Trade by H & L Pet Supplies Inc., 27 Kingston Crescent, Kitchener, Ontario N2B 2T6; Rolf C. Hagen Inc., 3225 Sartelon St. Laurent-Montreal Quebec H4R 1E8; in CANADA to the Book Trade by Vanwell Publishing Ltd., 1 Northrup Crescent, St. Catharines, Ontario L2M 6P5 ; in ENGLAND by T.F.H. Publications, PO Box 15, Waterlooville PO7 6BQ; in AUSTRALIA AND THE SOUTH PACIFIC by T.F.H. (Australia), Pty. Ltd., Box 149, Brookvale 2100 N.S.W., Australia; in NEW ZEALAND by Brooklands Aquarium Ltd. 5 McGiven Drive, New Plymouth, RD1 New Zealand; in Japan by T.F.H. Publications, Japan—Jiro Tsuda, 10-12-3 Ohjidai, Sakura, Chiba 285, Japan; in SOUTH AFRICA by Lopis (Pty) Ltd., P.O. Box 39127, Booysens, 2016, Johannesburg, South Africa. Published by T.F.H. Publications, Inc.

MANUFACTURED IN THE
UNITED STATES OF AMERICA
BY T.F.H. PUBLICATIONS, INC.

Dedicated to my wife of 42 years. Evelyn is more beautiful and wonderful than all the corals combined…and without stinging tentacles. I am indebted to Dr. Elizabeth M. Wood for the glossary; I have also relied upon her book as my major source of scientific data.

Caption Color Guide

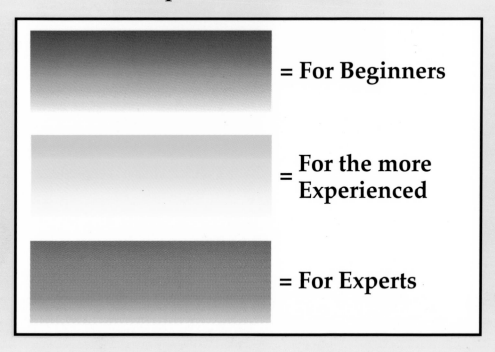

= For Beginners

= For the more Experienced

= For Experts

CONTENTS

INTRODUCTION TO CORALS IN THE MINI-REEF AQUARIUM

This book has taken 40 years to write. There are several important reasons for the delay. I had to answer the following questions:

1. Should corals be chopped off a reef and sold for aquarium purposes where they would surely die?

2. What popular and scientific name do you give a coral when scientists themselves can't readily identify them?

3. How do corals impact a mini-reef aquarium?

The fact that this book is now written indicates that I have satisfactorily answered these questions. But it took 40 years and visits to every major coral reef which was not too remote. These trips, most of which were reported in *Tropical Fish Hobbyist Magazine* as they took place, covered the reefs in Australia, New Guinea, Fiji, most of the major islands in between these places, Thailand, Singapore and Malaysia, Florida and the Caribbean Islands

including Cuba, Brazil, Guyana, Colombia, Peru, the Red Sea, Israel, the east coast of Africa, India, Pakistan and the Florida keys on both the Gulf of Mexico side and the Atlantic side. I have made the following conclusions to the three questions posed above:

1. In moderation, it is satisfactory to remove corals from their natural habitat. They may grow back quickly, be replaced by more aggressive corals, or may be grown in aqua-culture. I have never seen a "bald spot" in coral reefs, though I have seen many completely dead reefs as a result of water pollution either with chemicals or silt. I was shocked to see the coral atoll, Marau, completely ringed with dead, broken and decaying coral sites. It was a coral graveyard and disturbs me to this day.

2. Identifying corals, especially living corals removed from their natural range, is difficult if not

The author, Dr. Herbert R. Axelrod, on the island of Marau, in the South Pacific, photographing an anemonefish, *Amphiprion*, using sea fans (gorgonians) as a background.

Photo by Evelyn Axelrod.

impossible in many cases. I have been in the business of collecting and selling corals. We invented names for them based upon their color or their shape. Unfortunately, many species change shape or color depending upon changes in their habitat. In many cases we attributed scientific names to them based upon local "experts" who were not experts at all. We did identify corals by their skeletons; but that didn't help people buying living corals. To solve the name problem, we simply asked America's largest wholesaler/ importer of corals to supply us with the names he has given the corals, along with a photograph of that coral. This is about as good a system as possible. In almost all cases, I have tried to illustrate how that species lives in its own range and habitat. Unfortunately, the color of a coral is different in its natural depth, after it has been removed and shipped thousands of miles, and when the color photograph has been developed.

The bottom line is that there is NO positive identification of corals in many cases, without a scientist specializing in corals making the judgment. Keep in mind that many coral animals are community animals and, as such, the community itself has characteristics which are not visible when a single piece of coral is at hand. If you have a photo of the colony and a sample which can be soaked in chlorine or other bleach, so the skeleton can be studied, a scientist can readily identify the coral as to genus. The species is another story. Throughout the biological world, the definition of a species has always been arguable.

The author, Dr. Herbert R. Axelrod, diving on the recently murdered reef around the island of Marau. It had been killed by fishermen using cyanide.

3. Against my advice in the early days, hobbyists kept adding corals to their aquarium, gradually acquiring knowledge on how to care for them. To masquerade their efforts, they called the corals **living rocks**. It didn't seem that when the corals died, the whole tank was polluted. I guess the coral animals were eaten by the fishes or shrimps before they had a chance to pollute the tank.

So, after so many years of waffling, I have concluded that it is best to publish the truth as I see it. I don't know of anyone else who has collected corals throughout the world, sold them and studied them, and who is more authoritative as to their aquarium requirements. So here goes...

THE BIOLOGY OF CORALS IN THE MINI-REEF AQUARIUM

CORALS? WHAT ARE THEY?

When ordinary people hear the word *coral*, hard, limestone skeletons come to mind. To scientists, the term *coral* often means an animal or skeleton thereof, in the Order Scleractinia. All members of the Order Scleractinia produce hard, limestone skeletons. But there are soft corals, too.

The Scleractinia are divided into two groups. The **reef-building** Scleractinia are called *hermatypic*. They rely upon the sun to give them the energy to live via their symbiotic algae called *zooxanthellae*. The *ahermatypic* corals are non-reef building and live in the darkness or shade, usually deep in the ocean. They do not have these wonderful algae. These symbiotic algae belong to the genus

The forms in which corals grow:
A: Branching,
B: Massive,
C: Columnar,
D: Free-living,
E: Foliaceous, forming a whorl,
F: Laminar, forming a tier;
G: Encrusting.
A computer drawing by Jan Balon based upon a drawing by Geof Kelly and caption by Dr. J.E.N.Veron from his wonderful book Corals of Australia and the Indo-Pacific.

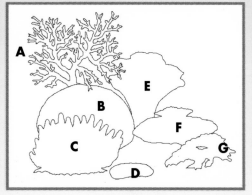

This is a successful mini-reef aquarium in the home of a beginner who has had only one year's experience but who relied heavily on the advice of his local aquarium shop. Photo by Isabelle Francais.

Symbiodinium. It is quite possible that more than one species of *Symbiodinium* is involved; it is also possible that other genera of algae may be involved as well.

There are also other organisms which build skeletons which look like the familiar corals. These are called *Nonscleractinian corals.* Another animal group are the *soft corals* which mostly have no skeleton at all!

Most corals are colonial animals

the water is neither too rough nor chemically polluted. As the land mass sinks into the ocean, the coral growth around the land mass usually stays where it is and gradually, completely or partially, encircles the area which has sunk.

Take Australia, for example. It has the most famous reef of corals called the *Barrier Reef.* Most reefs are *barriers* if some of the land mass is still exposed. Australia is

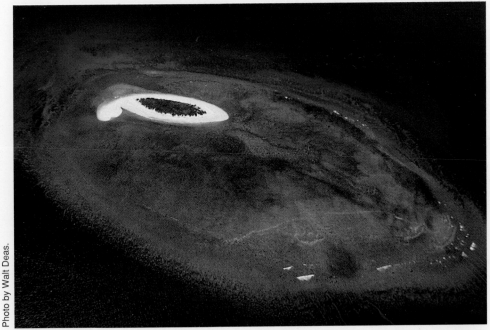

Photo by Walt Deas.

Erskine Island, Great Barrier Reef, Australia. You can see how the reef keeps moving in as the island sinks below sea level.

which exhibit tremendous variation from one range or habitat to another.

DISTRIBUTION OF CORALS AROUND THE WORLD

There are many large books which deal with the distribution of corals around the world. Essentially, corals exist on the side of every tropical island where

a large island. It has been dropping into the sea (the sea has been rising) over many thousands or millions of years. It has been doing this very slowly, thus allowing the development of the reef to proceed in a very efficient manner. The Great Barrier Reef of Australia is famous not only for the mass of beautiful corals, but for the color and variety of the

A reef on an unspoiled section in the Philippines. A reef is a restricted area with limited space for its inhabitants. This means the corals are in a constant battle for survival. They can't grow up as the waves will destroy them, they can't grow down as they are usually on a coral base, so they must expand sideways, fighting with their neighbors. Is it possible that their poisonous stinging cells are also used to clear the way for their growth? Photo by MP&C Piednoir, Aqua Press.

Photo by Walt Deas.

When tides are very low, coral reefs may actually be exposed to the air enabling tourists to walk on them (with protective shoes, of course).

other living things which go along with corals...the fishes, the algae, the invertebrates, the shrimps...altogether representing thousands of living species. The Great Barrier Reef is one of the largest things ever created by animals (humans included) with the possible exception of carbon fossil deposits which we know as coal, gas and oil. It certainly is the largest animal structure still living today. The Great Barrier Reef is about 1,200 miles long and runs along the northeast coast of Queensland, Australia. It

The Wistari Lagoon, Great Barrier Reef, showing the bottom being actively utilized by solitary corals. Solitary corals do well on the sandy bottoms of mini-reef aquariums.

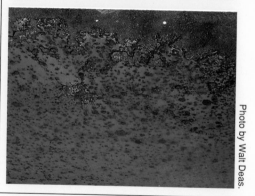

Photo by Walt Deas.

contains more than 2,500 individual huge reefs, the great majority of which are not barriers at all.

Collecting corals from the Great Barrier Reef is forbidden, yet the reef has been attacked by the Crown of Thorns starfish which have killed off large sections of the reef. Divers were used to kill the starfish and that seemed to control the threat.

As far as reefs go, the Great Barrier Reef is young, being only about two millions years old. Fossil remains indicate that reefs began forming 240 million years ago!

Photo by Walt Deas.

The Crown of Thorns starfish which eats coral animals. The *Acropora* upon which it was feeding is left stark white having been eaten down to its skeleton!

Having re-visited coral reefs over 40 years, I can see that the reefs have either flourished or failed. Living in Key West, Florida, I have the opportunity of seeing what happened to the reefs there. Like many natural crops, the reefs have their good years and their bad years. It didn't seem to have any effect when they banned coral collecting along Florida's coast. I am against reef destruction ANYPLACE in the world.

As luxurious as the Great Barrier Reef is, the Philippine Islands have twice as many species and easily twice as many miles of reef. Without regulation at all, the Philippine Islands are the source of most corals, marine invertebrates and fishes. Unfortunately, the use of cyanide to collect coral fishes is taking its toll on all the coral animals.

The Maldive Islands, which I fairly thoroughly examined, are also extremely rich in coral and coral fishes. Fortunately, the Maldives are not off limits for collecting either fishes or corals.

Corals are fragile but when years of them build themselves into a reef, they can sink ships. The world's coral reefs are mute testimony to the tragedies of ships storm-driven onto reefs.

symbiotic relationship of coral polyps and algae. It is the skeletons of corals which accumulate and which are cemented together due to algae.

The algae are single-celled plants which live symbiotically within the coral polyps' cells. (*Symbiosis* is when two animals of different origin cooperate for the benefit of both of them.) These algae are called **zooxanthellae**. They belong to the single-celled brown plants which are known as **dinoflagellates**. Normally these dinoflagellates are food for newly

The reef edge, being constantly pounded by the surging surf, is practically lifeless as far as corals go. All the corals are growing on the declining edge of the reef below the water level.

Generally speaking, reef-building corals are found 30° north and south of the equator where the temperature averages 68°F. or higher.

CORALS NEED ALGAE

Huge coral buildups which can be miles deep and perhaps miles wide (the thickest coral reef was measured at 3,000 feet thick) are essentially dependent upon the

Green Island, Great Barrier Reef, has had a channel blasted through its protective ring to make it accessible for docking fishing boats. It also made it accessible to coral-eating fishes!

hatched shrimp and newly hatched fishes. They are very helpful as food, but sometimes they have an unusual bloom and form what is called the *red tide*. They rob the oxygen from the water and many higher animals and plants die as a result. Since shellfish like oysters, clams and mussels filter the water for food, feeding mainly on dinoflagellates, they die if the dinoflagellates are toxic. They also can cause shellfish poisoning which kills the shellfish and makes people sick if they eat the dead or dying shellfish.

A coral cay (key) which is a coral island on the Great Barrier Reef. Locales like this abound in a plentiful coral life.

Photo by Walt Deas.

Photo by Walt Deas.

A reef exposed at low tide but protected from the surge of the surf because it is really in a lagoon. A great place for corals and fishes but there is no way to get down to see them!

Specific algae have the ability to penetrate the coral's tissues and without them most of the reef-building corals would not exist as we know them today.

For this reason coral colonies are found increasingly abundant and luxurious the closer they are to the sun. If algae-bearing corals are kept in the dark, they die within 60-180 days. In clear coral seas they normally grow best within 100 feet of the surface of the water. They are almost never building reefs deeper than 150 feet ...and it is almost impossible to find any reef building species deeper than 275 feet of ocean depth.

But not every coral uses zooxanthellae. We use the term *hermatypic* for those corals that do use the zooxanthellae. That's what gives them the ability to build reefs. The *ahermatypic* corals have no zooxanthellae, thus they cannot build reefs.

The zooxanthellae help the hermatypic corals in several ways. Almost all of the organic carbon they produce (about 95%) is

Heron Island and Wistari Reef, Great Barrier Reef, gives some idea of the huge variety of coral habitats available for exploitation by coral flower animals. That's why the Great Barrier Reef has so many coral varieties.

Photo by Walt Deas.

Photo by Walt Deas.

The beginning of a new coral reef! This reef is starting on the coral floor with a sand base. In 10,000 years it might be 50 feet high underwater!

They are inexpensive.

When corals reproduce, their larvae are also infected with zooxanthellae, thus enabling them to duplicate their parents' reef building capacity. The infection of the larvae usually takes place at fertilization. Thus there is one fertilized egg (which is one cell) in which there is one alga (*alga* is the singular of *algae*). Generally, as the egg divides eventually forming a new coral animal, each cell is infected with just one alga.

absorbed as food by the coral polyp. In reef building, the zooxanthellae use sunlight for photosynthesis and this assists the corals in building their limestone skeletons which eventually become parts of the reef. The zooxanthellae are able to use the deadly ammonia produced by the corals' metabolic processes for their own energy requirements. Ammonia released by living aquarium inhabitants in both freshwater and saltwater can quickly kill all living vertebrates in that particular aquarium. Ammonia testing kits are recommended for all aquarists.

The edge of a reef, where the coral growth begins, is opportunistic for divers who can walk to the beginning of the reef instead of having to swim there!

WHAT DO CORALS EAT?

Corals have two sources of food.

Photo by Walt Deas.

North Reef, Great Barrier Reef, showing the rare habitat possibilities for protected coral growth.

About 95% of their food is supplied by the organic waste excreted by the zooxanthellae. The balance are living prey or debris which swim or float into the area in which the coral polyps are waving, get stunned by the tentacles and are then captured by other tentacles until they are swallowed. Sometimes the coral polyp does not like the taste of a morsel of food, even after it has stung it into immobility. Unsavory food is simply released. Coral polyps can also be tricked into

Photo by Walt Deas.

eating cotton or paper which has been soaked in brine shrimp decay.

Ahermatypic corals do not have zooxanthellae, thus they cannot get 95% of their food from algae. Instead they are all predatory carnivores which eat anything they can paralyze with their stinging tentacles. This includes fish, worms, shrimps and sea urchins. THIS IS IMPORTANT TO KNOW FOR THE MINI-REEF HOBBYIST!

Don't believe those writers who proclaim corals with algae can live without additional food. Maybe they can live without you feeding them, but they must get food either through the absorption of organic and inorganic materials from sea water, from collecting floating debris in the water (like fish feces), or from eating microscopic foods like bacteria.

In their natural habitat some corals only expand their tentacles during the night when zooplankton are most abundant. Others may extend their tentacles during the day, some both day and night. To make matters even more confusing, I have observed the same species in two different tanks opening their tentacles at different times...some at night, some during the day and some during both periods.

The lesson to be learned for mini-reefers is this: Feed the corals daily. Use zooplankton if you can grow it, collect it or buy it. Try newly hatched brine shrimp nauplii, *Artemia* species. Most pet shops sell the eggs and they are easy to hatch. These live for many hours in a marine tank. The filters must be turned off during feeding. The fish and anemones will eat them as well. To ensure that the corals get their fair share, direct a bright spotlight onto the coral head while the rest of the tank is dark. The brine shrimp nauplii (nauplii means *newly hatched*) are attracted to the light where they have a better chance of being snared by the tentacles of the corals.

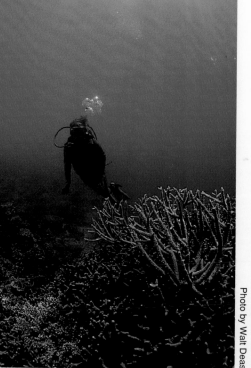

Photo by Walt Deas.

Staghorn coral, *Acropora,* amid *Porites cylindrica* fighting for its turf. *Porites* are famous (in mini-reef aquariums) for the worms which infest them.

THE GREEN GORGONIAN, OR GREEN QUILL, *MURICEA* SPECIES, IS A VERY PRETTY GORGONIAN FOR ADVANCED MINI-REEFERS. IT IS BEING FARMED AND IS AVAILABLE AT RELATIVELY LOW PRICES. PHOTO BY ISABELLE FRANCAIS. 6 HOURS FLUORESCENT LIGHTING; CONSTANT, MODERATE WATER MOVEMENT; REQUIRES FEEDING; NOT FOR BEGINNERS.

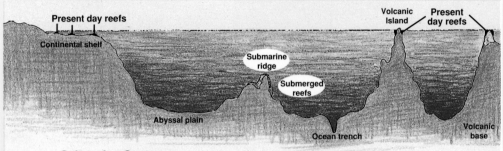

Submarine Contours

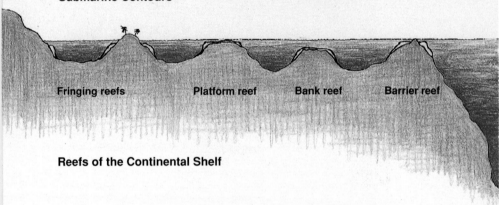

Reefs of the Continental Shelf

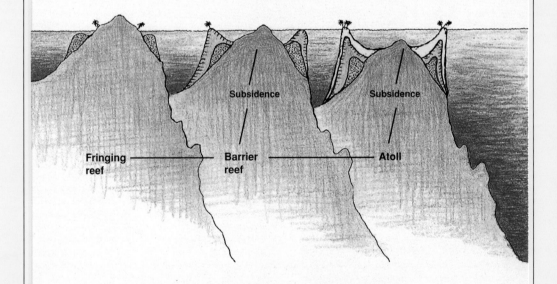

Oceanic Reefs and Darwin's Theory of Atoll Formation

There are two possibilities of error: Feeding corals that don't eat, or not feeding corals that do require food. Obviously, you want to make the first error because the other inhabitants of the mini-reef aquarium will eat the brine shrimp nauplii if the corals do not.

HOW DO CORALS GROW?

Corals have existed for 240

especially such plants as water lilies and potatoes. The coral colonies, when large, have thousands or even millions of individual coral polyps, all waving their tentacles to capture a morsel. The polyps live a long time. No one knows how long, but since their growth can be measured, a simple arithmetic calculation tells the tale. Take *Acropora*. It produces individual

Photo by Walt Deas on the Great Barrier Reef.

This can happen in your mini-reef aquarium. The *Porites cylindrica* has killed off all the *Acropora* except for this last piece.

million years. The Scleractinia have utilized their symbiotic relationship with the algae very well. This has enabled them to build huge reefs and large colonies. The colonies are usually formed by *budding*. This asexual manner of reproduction is used by many plants,

skeletons to protect each polyp. These skeletons are called *corallites*. The coral *Acropora hyacinthus* can grow up to 4 inches per year under favorable circumstances. Thus a 5 feet long *A. hyacinthus* can be 15 years old!

HOW DO CORALS REPRODUCE?

Corals may very well be the world's champion breeders. They use almost every known way of breeding and reproducing. The asexual means are well known. These are budding, branching, splitting and escaping."Escaping?" Yes, some coral polyps have the ability to leave their corallite shells and look for a new home. This ensures allows for genetic variation and wide dispersion. This is interesting because most corals, when sexually mature, cannot move from their corallites. They are stuck in one small area and cannot make physical contact with other corals.

Many coral polyps are bisexual. They have the sexual organs of both sexes. They might even fertilize themselves! This is not

A SMALL *FUNGIA ACTINIFORMIS* ON A STALK ABOUT TO BECOME DETACHED AND FREE-LIVING. 8 HOURS FLUORESCENT LIGHTING; CONSTANT, MODERATE WATER MOVEMENT; MUST BE FED.

that the coral can still exist if their colony is threatened in any way.

The most fascinating reproductive techniques practiced by corals are sexual. Sexual reproduction has many advantages over asexual reproduction. When sperms and eggs are produced and released it unique. There are many animals (worms) and flowers which have both gonads (sex organs).

But there are usually two general types of sexual reproduction. The males release sperm which float into the female's reproductive cavity for internal fertilization, or the female releases her eggs about the same time the male releases his sperm, hoping they will meet before the strong tides disperse them. Their timing is a natural miracle!

In studies done on the Great Barrier Reef, it was found that moon should they use as their clock?? Simple. They await the most rapid increase in the temperature of the water. This is right after winter. Thus the biological clock signals the corals. It has been estimated

ACROPORA HYACINTHUS REPRODUCES SEXUALLY BY BIOLOGICAL CLOCK; NEEDS METAL HALIDE BUT BREAK IN WITH 12 HOURS OF INTENSE FLUORESCENT LIGHT; HEAVY WATER FLOW; DEFINITELY NOT FOR BEGINNERS; EXPERIMENT WITH FEEDING BRINE SHRIMP.

the eggs and sperm, of certain species of coral, were released just as it gets dark. But to make sure that they get the correct day in which to release their gametes (eggs and sperm) they follow the moon. The corals wait for a full moon, for at full moon the tides are highest and weakest. But there are 13 full moons per year. Which full that half of all the corals on the Great Barrier Reef release their sperm and eggs when it gets dark, five days after the full moon in the late spring.

Some day, aquaculturists will collect the fertilized coral eggs and grow them in ponds, tubs or vats. Then they can be produced cheaper and we can all have clear consciences.

Books can be (and have been) written about the complete biology of corals. Their structure, their physiology, the definition of their reef-building characteristics, but that is not the function of this book. For that kind of information you must read **CORALS OF THE WORLD by Dr. Elizabeth M. Wood (ISBN 0-86622-657-5; TFH number is H-1049).**

CORALS
OF THE WORLD
DR. ELIZABETH M. WOOD

If you are interested in the entire world of hard corals, get a copy of Dr. Wood's thrilling book. Pet shops carry this book.

BREEDING CORALS IN THE AQUARIUM

If you are able to keep your corals alive in your mini-reef aquarium, you should be able to breed them too. Sexual reproduction in a mini-reef aquarium is possible. The surest way to grow corals is by vegetative reproduction. In the following discussions of individual species or genera, breeding hints are given. In general, here is what I have done in the past.

Keeping in mind that a piece of coral, regardless of its size, is usually made up of many small corallites, you only need a few corallites to start a new colony. So I would break off a small piece of coral and take it home. The piece would never be less than 3 inches in any dimension, nor would it be larger than 10 inches. Carrying the coral home requires skill. I usually plant the base in a bear-trap type of device. The clamp would hold the coral fragment in an upright position, while the heavy base of the clamp would maintain it in this position during transport.

I have also been successful in attaching a piece of coral to a piece of styrofoam and floating it in a plastic bag about 25% filled with ocean water, but deep enough for the styrofoam to float. I then filled the rest of the bag with oxygen. If you are buying your supplies from a local aquarium shop ask him to show you how he receives the corals he buys and learn from this. He will also be able to sell you the necessary styrofoam boxes and plastic bags you'll need to bring your corals home. Make sure it is legal to collect corals before you break off a piece to take home. If you don't chop off too big a piece, the coral usually regenerates itself in a few months and you'd never know someone took off a piece.

Once you get home, situate the coral as far from strong light as possible, even if you have to drill a hole in your living rock in which to insert the new coral. If

A *WORD OF CAUTION:* CORALS CAN STING YOU. ALWAYS WEAR HEAVY GLOVES WHEN HANDLING CORALS AND BE CAREFUL THAT YOUR WRISTS ARE NOT EXPOSED TO STINGING TENTACLES.

all else fails, just lay it on the bottom in fine sand, with the corallites facing the light. Gradually move the new coral to the recommended light intensity.

In many cases it is not necessary to break off a piece of coral. You usually can find new, small growths attached to dead fragments in the sand around the coral mass.

During storage or transport, corals should be isolated from all other living things. They should be protected from constant rubbing against the sides of a plastic bag or anything else. They should have plenty of clean water. Their water should be changed daily, if possible. Shipping corals worldwide is the business of professionals. If, for any reason, you have to move corals over long distances, ask your experienced marine fish dealer for help.

Corals should be planted as far apart as possible so they can grow and reproduce...as you get experience in handling them. This is what a one year beginner's mini-reef should look like.

Photo by R. Wederich.

This marine tank is on display in Nancy, France (at the University). It shows the ultimate in mini-reef aquarium care. The tank is 4 feet deep. Photo courtesy of Nancy Aquarium, Dr. Denis Terver.

WHICH CORAL IS THAT?

It is fairly difficult to identify a piece of coral found in a pet shop or your home aquarium. It is often very difficult for a scientist to identify a coral even if he sees it on a reef where he at least knows its origin.

If you want to see how difficult it is, and you have some scuba (**s**elf **c**ontained **u**nderwater **b**reathing **a**pparatus) experience, examine any reef slope. Those corals which are around the top of the slope, constantly exposed to strong wave and tidal action, are usually tough little specimens, very solidly developed. As you go deeper and deeper, the coral colonies become more delicate, probably more colorful, and much more variable in shape and size. If you keep going down the slope and eventually reach the twilight zone, these very same corals have

once again changed their shapes. They are now huge, wide tables, or delicately branching structures, formations too delicate for any wave action at all! This is

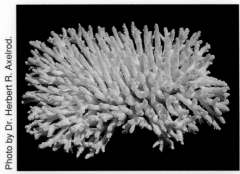

Porcupine *Acropora* was sold in curio shops in the Caribbean during the 1950's. Now all hard coral collecting is strictly forbidden in most of the Caribbean and Gulf coasts of Florida and Central America.

the SAME species, mind you. When you buy it from a dealer, he very frequently offers another name for a different form of the same species.

ALMOST ALL CORAL SPECIES HAVE VARIABLE GROWTH FORMS AND CORALLITE CONSTRUCTION. When there is any doubt about a species, the coral scientists depend upon the bleached skeleton of the coral at hand. These skeletons are very reliable as to genus. Add to this complication the fact that fossil corals must also be considered, and you have some idea of the problem.

How then can mini-reefers identify a piece of coral?

NOT FOR BEGINNERS; 12 HOURS FLUORESCENT THEN METAL HALIDE LIGHTING; NEEDS ROOM TO GROW; MODERATE TO HEAVY WATER MOVEMENT; NO FEEDING IF KEPT WITH FISHES.

Purple Acropora, *Acropora tenuis*, also known as Dead-man's Fingers when it is sold as a skeleton (shown below).

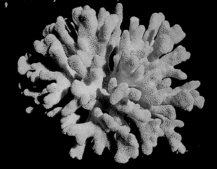

Truly, no one can be certain of the identification of a piece of coral without knowing where it came from, at what depth and having skeletonized it. The best way is to identify them from photographs taken in their natural habitat. Photographs of tank specimens makes writing a coral book simple since you don't have to travel around the world, photograph the specimen, collect it, then skeletonize it to verify its identification.

IN THIS BOOK MOST OF THE IDENTIFICATIONS HAVE BEEN MADE FROM ACTUAL LIVING SPECIMENS IN THEIR NATURAL RANGE. The photographs are of specimens living in their natural range. There are NO identifications made from aquarium specimens. To make it a bit easier, the common names have been applied by the shape or color of a given specimen. It is probable that different species have the same common name, but this is the case with fishes, flowers, trees, birds and just about anything else that forms a recognizable group.

It doesn't really matter whether you have correctly identified the coral or not. You must have an open mind about its care. Since the same coral species can live at different light levels and different depths, obviously its needs in the mini-reef aquarium vary. You have to experiment with water movement, water temperature, light and feedings. Of course if you have more than one kind of coral, you have seriously complicated the problem. But if you persist, you'll learn. If a coral doesn't seem to be doing too well

Advanced mini-reef aquarium with corals, anemones and anemone fishes, *Amphiprion percula*.

Well-established mini-reef aquarium with huge anemones and a pair of anemone fishes which spawned in the mini-reef tank but the young died of starvation after they absorbed their yolk sacs.

in a particular spot in your mini-reef aquarium, move it to another depth where it will get more or less light and water movement. Often the coral changes its needs to accommodate its environment. It does this in nature, so why shouldn't it do the same thing in your aquarium? That could be the subject of another book. As much as we'd like to think of our mini-reef aquarium as a real reef, it just is not. The dynamics of a mini-reef aquarium vary from house to house, tank to tank. You have to understand principles in order to achieve success.

Each coral genus to be discussed will have hints about keeping it alive and healthy in a mini-reef aquarium. That's about the best we can do to guide you.

One last tip. Corals do better when they are kept with fishes. Bits of fish food and fish droppings are usually turned into food for the corals. In this sense, the corals are scavengers.

The perfect mini-reef aquarium.

Photo by R. Wederich.

CLOSED BRAIN CORAL,
PINEAPPLE CORAL, BRAIN CORAL, MOON CORAL, MOONSTONE, MODERN AND HONEYCOMB CORAL

THE GENUS *FAVIA*

Honeycomb is the best name because it is a translation of the scientific name *Favia*.

We start with this genus because it has such a wide range from the east coast of the U.S, down to Rio de Janeiro, Brazil, across to parts of the west coast of Africa, across from South Africa and the entire east coast of Africa, the Red Sea, all around the warm waters of Australia and onto the reefs in much of the Pacific without touching the American west coast.

These are very adaptable species. In nature they only feed at night. Their polyps are tube-shaped and fringed like a moustache with clear tentacles which quickly react to anything

touching them...including strong light. Using a flashbulb underwater in 1955, I photographed a beautiful mass of *Favia*, with their tentacles fully extended. It was beautiful. I took another photo a minute later and all the tentacles had been retracted. Had they reacted to the light?

The genus was originally constructed by Oken in 1815 and was based upon Esper's description in 1795 of a Caribbean species he called *Madrepora fragum*. There are more than 70 species and equally as many sub-species, depending upon the systematist (the scientist who is interested in corals' names). There is no uniformity of reproduction nor of feeding habits within the genus

The colonies are usually about 5-6 feet in diameter and shaped like a table or a dome. The tentacles fringe the entire polyp; polyps only come out at night. Many species have clear tentacles with pigmented tips. The genus *Favia* is frequently confused with the genera *Favites* and *Barabattoia*. Like most corals, they are difficult to identify since

Photo by Dr. Herbert R. Axelrod.

FAVIA PALLIDA, ALSO CALLED THE MOON, BRAIN OR BOULDER CORAL. OK FOR BEGINNERS; MODERATE WATER FLOW, FLUORESCENT LIGHTING 4-12 HOURS DAILY, THEN METAL HALIDE AFTER A MONTH OF 4 FLUORESCENTS; FEED BRINE SHRIMP; MODEST WATER FLOW; HIGHLY RECOMMENDED.

they vary tremendously in color.

They are hardy in the mini-reef aquarium and grow quickly because they are mostly shallow water corals to begin with. They thrive on brine shrimp though they need not be fed if they have fishes in the same mini-reef aquarium. They often reproduce by budding. Small polyps develop like pimples and gradually enlarge until they fall off. These can be gathered and attached to the live rock in a fashion that suits your decorative tastes. It usually takes 75 days between the time you notice the pimple to the time it falls off. Then it takes another few months to attach itself to the position in which you place it. While most of the species are hermaphrodites, with both sex organs being present in the same polyp, the more usual reproductive style in vegetative. The example cited in the previous section, subtitled *How Do Corals Reproduce?*, details the sexual reproductive behavior of the corals in the genus *Favia*.

The name *Favia* derives from the Latin *favus* which means *honeycomb*, referring to the geometrical appearance of the corallites.

The *Favia* species all look alike when they extend their tentacles, usually at night.

ORANGE CLOSED BRAIN CORAL
FAVIA PALLIDA
Dana, 1846

The center of distribution is the Fiji Islands where they are very common. Their color is an extremely variable cream, orange, tan or green. The opening of the corallite (calice) is green or brown. It ranges from East Africa to Australia and as far north as the Red Sea. It is a very commonly exported species from Africa, Israel and Saudi Arabia. It does well almost anyplace in the mini-reef aquarium provided it gets light. Several paperback books on corals in the aquarium are clearly incorrect when they cite the ovoid characteristics of the corallite. Most corallites are circular unless their common wall has been distorted by the more rapid growth of its connecting sister.

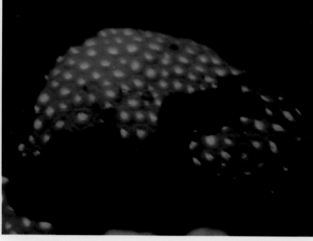

Photo by Dr. Herbert R. Axelrod.

Favia **fluorescent under UV light. By putting a UV lamp in your top hood reflector, you can leave it on for a few hours at night. The *Favia* zooxanthellae seem to enjoy it.**

FAVIA PALLIDA 8-10 HOURS WITH 4 FLUORESCENTS; MODERATE WATER MOTION; NEEDS GROWING ROOM; CAN BE FED.

Under proper conditions, this coral grows quickly, so leave plenty of room around it.

BROWN or GREEN CLOSED BRAIN CORAL

FAVIA STELLIGERA

Dana, 1846

This fairly rare species originates in Fiji but is found as far away as the Red Sea, Malaysia, Hawaii and Australia. It is an easy coral to recognize because the corallites are very uniform and the calice (opening) is small.

They do best in a well lit situation with moderate water movement to bring food into its reach. It grows slowly, if at all, unless properly fed. It can subsist without special feedings and low light level, but then it turns brown or green. Under proper lighting it is pinkish orange.

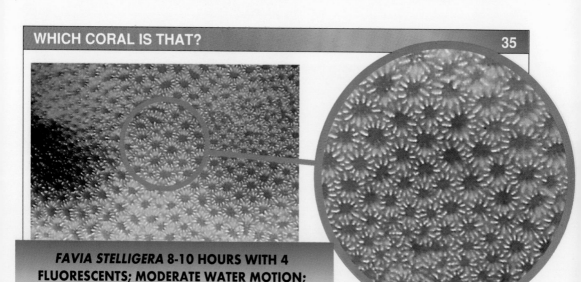

FAVIA STELLIGERA 8-10 HOURS WITH 4 FLUORESCENTS; MODERATE WATER MOTION; NEEDS GROWING ROOM; CAN BE FED.

TAN CLOSED BRAIN CORAL

FAVIA LAXA
Klunzinger, 1879

This rare species, not abundant anywhere, has been showing up in shipments from the Red Sea. It ranges throughout Australian reefs on both the east and west coasts, and throughout the south Pacific.

It is easily confused with *Favia stelligera*, but *stelligera* has more diminutive corallites and heavier septa. This species reproduces easily from small pieces about 4 inches (smallest dimension) chopped off the main colony, though larger pieces are being shipped from the Red Sea. Klunzinger described this species from a Red Sea specimen more than 100 years ago. It loves light and appreciates monthly feedings of newly hatched brine shrimp, but feed weekly if there are no fishes in the mini-reef aquarium with this coral.

FAVIA LAXA 12 HOURS OF LIGHT WITH 4 FLUORESCENTS; MODERATE WATER MOVEMENT; SHOULD BE FED.

Photos by Walt Deas.

FAVIA HELIANTHOIDES, THE GOLDEN CLOSED BRAIN CORAL, IS IDEAL FOR THE BEGINNER. LIGHT TO HEAVY LIGHTING; MODEST WATER MOTION AND SLOW GROWTH.

GOLDEN CLOSED BRAIN CORAL

FAVIA HELIANTHOIDES
Wells, 1954

A widely distributed species found on both coasts of Australia, through the south Pacific especially the Marshall and Mariana Islands and throughout the Coral Sea atolls.

This species, though widely distributed, is rare in nature. A close inspection of its polyps indicate that corallites are neither uniform nor circular. The smallest corallites start out round but change to oval shapes as they get larger. They are also widely spread over the colony's surface. It certainly doesn't live up to the *honeycomb* description of the genus name *Favia*.

It enjoys random feedings of brine shrimp nauplii but gets along without feeding if maintained in the mini-reef aquarium with fishes. They are usually yellow, light tan or gold in color.

Photos by Dr. Elizabeth M. Wood and Walt Deas.

FAVIA FAVUS, THE CHAMELEON CLOSED BRAIN CORAL, IS THE IDEAL CORAL FOR BEGINNERS. LIGHT TO HEAVY LIGHTING; MODEST WATER MOVEMENTS AND SLOW GROWTH.

CHAMELEON CLOSED BRAIN CORAL

FAVIA FAVUS
Forskal, 1775

An extremely abundant species found in huge colonies from the Red Sea (where it was first discovered by scientists) throughout the Coral Sea to the Marshall Islands thence to Australia where it is found on almost every coral reef on either (or both) coasts.

Its corallites are not round but more egg-shaped and very closely packed together. When fully expanded at night, their tentacles overlap and cover the entire surface of the colony. It is often the dominant species in most reefs where it is found. It appears in just about every color known to corals. The colors change in the aquarium probably due to the wave lengths of the light available, the diet and its contentment. The colors are very variable in their natural habitat as well. They should be planted as close to the light source as possible; they grow quickly and are aggressive, crowding out more slow growing and timid coral species.

Photos by Walt Deas.

FAVIA *SPECIOSA*, THE GREEN BROWN CLOSED BRAIN CORAL, IS EXCELLENT FOR BEGINNERS. LIGHT OR HEAVY LIGHTING, MODEST WATER MOVEMENT AND SLOW GROWTH.

GREEN BROWN CLOSED BRAIN CORAL

FAVIA SPECIOSA
Dana, 1846

This is a widely distributed coral found from the Red Sea, around east African coral sites to the Great Barrier Reef of Australia, around all of Australia on both coasts, throughout the Coral Sea and in most south Pacific atolls. It is often imported under the name *Favia pallida*, because *pallida* is so varied in color. I have never seen a single-colored *speciosa*.

These may be difficult corals to maintain in the mini-reef aquarium. They do best not quite so close to the strong lights necessary for most coral's survival. They also appreciate some brine shrimp unless there are quite a few fish in with them.

They are truly beautiful in the aquarium if kept isolated from more aggressive species of coral. They are usually imported from

Photos by Walt Deas and Dr. Elizabeth M. Wood.

FAVIA MATTHAII, **THE BROWN OR GREY CLOSED BRAIN CORAL, IS EXCELLENT FOR BEGINNING MINI-REEFERS. LIGHT OR HEAVY LIGHTING, MODEST WATER MOVEMENT AND SLOW GROWTH.**

the Red Sea, Indonesia and perhaps the Philippines.

BROWN or GREY CLOSED BRAIN CORAL

FAVIA MATTHAII
Vaughan, 1918

This species is common when it is found at all. It is usually not found very close to the surface which indicates it doesn't like violent water agitation nor light which is too intense. It is not very colorful but it does have a contrast between the dark polyp centers and the surrounding calice (a *calice* is that part of the corallite which is visible). It does very well in the aquarium and the coral polyps are tightly packed, one against the other. The uneven, saw-tooth septa (*septa* are the radiating parts of the corallite wall which extend above the edge of the corallite) are characteristic and unique, making identification easy. Once it settles in, it becomes quite hardy and grows aggressively. Feeding is not necessary if maintained with fishes in the same mini-reef aquarium.

Photos by Walt Deas.

FAVIA ROTUMANA, THE CLOSED BRAIN CORAL, IS EXCELLENT FOR BEGINNERS. LIGHT OR HEAVY LIGHTING, MODERATE WATER MOVEMENT AND SLOW GROWTH.

CLOSED BRAIN CORAL

FAVIA ROTUMANA
Gardiner, 1899

(usually named after the color of the individual specimen, such as BROWN CLOSED BRAIN CORAL, etc.)

I found this species in huge quantities in the Fiji Islands from which they were exported from 1952 until about 1975 when exports of live rocks were prohibited.

Because they are so colorful and different colors are often found in the same reef, they are popular export items and are being supplied from the southern China Sea. They are found all around Australia, across the south Pacific to American Samoa, to many of the unidentified atolls which dot the South Pacific.

When well fed, the *rotumana* have very contrasting colors. The corallites usually contrast with the soft polyp. They like strong light and do not require feeding if kept with fishes in the mini-reef aquarium. I have found that they grow faster and are more colorful when fed brine shrimp at night (one night a week is enough). Those brine shrimp which are uneaten by the *rotumana* are quickly consumed by the fishes once there is enough light in the aquarium for them to see the shrimp.

PINEAPPLE CORALS

THE GENUS *FAVITES*

This genus was constructed in 1807 by Link based upon a coral he named *Favites astrinus*. He was unable to describe the origin of the specimen.

The *Favites* are closely related to the *Favia*. They usually occupy the same ecological niche which is turbid, shallow water. They are all night feeders whose polyps are finger-like when they are extended at night. The term *favites* means *like a honeycomb*. The corallites are fused to each other, thus sharing common walls with the adjacent polyps. The walls are not uniform, thus the surface of the colony is rough. Each corallite is slightly different from the adjacent one both in shape and in elevation. The calice (visible) corallite walls range in diameter from almost one inch (25 mm) to about $1/4$ inch (6 mm). Almost 35 species have been described because of the great variability of the uneven walls, but when separated into pieces for shipment and culture in the mini-reef aquarium, the new colony often loses the characteristics of the natural colony, thus bringing into question many of the so-called species. There are probably only a dozen valid species (not to mention sub-species) and most of the species are found in Australia's Great Barrier Reef from which specimens may NOT be collected commercially.

They are called *pineapple corals* because they form roundish colonies, about the size of a large pineapple or basketballs, and have a brown color. But many dealers buy and sell them as moon or brain corals. The literature is very confusing when it comes to popular names of all corals, but especially *Favites*.

The color of the corals in the genus *Favites* varies with the lighting. A strong actinic lighting brings out colors that are abnormal when viewed with normal room light. The non-Australian species of *Favites* are the most widely imported.

Photo by Walt Deas.

FAVITES, THE PINEAPPLE CORALS, SPECIES ARE EXCELLENT FOR BEGINNING MINI-REEFERS. THESE CORALS REQUIRE LIGHT TO HEAVY LIGHTING; MODERATE WATER MOVEMENT AND THEY GROW SLOWLY.

Photos by Walt Deas.

FAVITES FLEXUOSA, THE PINEAPPLE CORAL, IS EXCELLENT FOR THE BEGINNER. IT REQUIRES FROM LIGHT TO HEAVY LIGHTING, MODERATE WATER MOVEMENT AND IS SLOW GROWING.

PINEAPPLE, GREEN MOON, BROWN MOON

FAVITES FLEXUOSA
Dana, 1846

The type locality for this species is the Fiji Islands where I found them in huge colonies (1955). They occur in green and brown and are very popular mini-reef aquarium specimens. They are widely distributed in nature being found all around Australia, through the Coral Sea and from the Red Sea to Fiji. Quite a wide distribution! They are very abundant wherever they are found which illustrates their aggressiveness. They grow quickly in the mini-reef aquarium, so give them plenty of room. If you don't feed them they grow more slowly, but they should be fed brine shrimp if they are not kept with fishes.

Photos by Walt Deas.

FAVITES ABDITA, THE GREEN MOON CORAL, IS EXCELLENT FOR BEGINNERS. IT REQUIRES LOW TO HEAVY LIGHTING, MODERATE WATER MOVEMENT AND IS SLOW GROWING.

GREEN MOON, GREEN PINEAPPLE

FAVITES ABDITA
Ellis & Solander, 1786

This is a widely distributed species found from the Red Sea all the way to Australia, including Samoa. It is commonly shipped from the Red Sea and is easily confused with *Favites flexuosa* but has much smaller and more uniform corallites. These corals form massive heads 3-4 feet in diameter. They have sharp teeth and I have often slashed my legs when swimming around them to catch small fishes! They seem to have stinging tentacles to which some aquarists may be allergic, so only handle them with thick gloves.

They are beautiful under actinic light and do well under almost all mini-reef conditions. They often become very dark when conditions are not too favorable.

Photos by Walt Deas.

FAVITES HALICORA, THE MOSS MOON CORAL, IS A GREAT CORAL FOR THE BEGINNING MINI-REEFER. LIGHT TO MODERATE LIGHTING, MODERATE WATER MOVEMENT AND SLOW GROWTH MAKE THIS AN EASY CORAL TO REAR.

MOSS MOON,
FADED PINEAPPLE

FAVITES HALICORA
Ehrenberg, 1834

This coral was identified more than 150 years ago from specimens collected at the Red Sea. Since that time rich colonies have been uncovered all across the Pacifiç, the Coral Sea and the entire island continent of Australia where corals normally grow.

This species is often confused with *Favites abdita* but it has thicker walls and less sloping corallites.

This is a rare coral even in nature. It is non-aggressive and suffers when kept with more aggressive species. It loves light and, when not subjected to competition, it grows into huge colonies which usually are rounded.

In the mini-reef aquarium they have few special requirements except strong actinic light and ample feeding through fishes' waste or from brine shrimp. When they do well, they usually flourish; when they don't grow, they die.

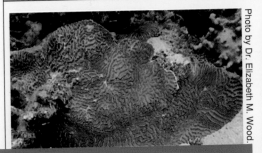

Photo by Dr. Elizabeth M. Wood.

Photo by Dr. Elizabeth M. Wood.

GROOVED BRAIN, BOULDER, GROOVED BOULDER, BRAIN, *OULOPHYLLIA CRISPA*, LAMARCK, 1816. FOUND FROM THE RED SEA TO THE GREAT BARRIER REEF OF AUSTRALIA, *OULOPHYLLIA* IS VERY POPULAR IN THE MINI-REEF AQUARIUM. THEY ARE EASY TO KEEP WITH LIGHT WATER MOVEMENT, 10 HOURS OF INTENSE FLUORESCENT LIGHTING PER DAY, AND LIGHT FEEDINGS OF NEWLY HATCHED BRINE SHRIMP ONCE A WEEK WHEN THEIR TENTACLES ARE EXPANDED. THEY ARE NOT OVERLY AGGRESSIVE BUT ALL CORALS SHOULD BE GIVEN ROOM TO GROW AND EXTEND THEIR TENTACLES.

GROOVED BRAIN, *OULOPHYLLIA CRISPA*, LAMARCK, 1816. THIS IS THE TYPICAL BRAIN CORAL MODE; THE ADJACENT PHOTO SHOWS THE CORAL EXPANDING IN AN AGGRESSIVE MANNER BECAUSE THERE IS NOTHING TO IMPEDE ITS GROWTH. THE SAME IS TRUE IN THE MINI-REEF AQUARIUM. IF YOU WANT A LOT OF CORALS, PLANT THEM CLOSE TOGETHER AND WATCH THEM ATTACK THEIR MORE DOCILE NEIGHBORS. PEACE IS ACHIEVED WITH PLENTY OF LIVING ROOM...A COMMON REQUIREMENT FOR MOST LIVING THINGS.

Photo by Walt Deas.

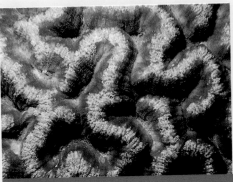

Photo by Walt Deas.

DENTED PURPLE BRAIN, *SYMPHYLLIA RADIANS*, EDWARDS & HAIME, 1849. THIS IS A VERY PREVALENT SPECIES IN THE MALDIVE ISLANDS WHERE I FOUND THEM ON EVERY REEF I INVESTIGATED. THEY DID WELL IN MY MINI-REEF AQUARIUM. THEY NEED 10 HOURS OF STRONG LIGHT, VERY LITTLE WATER MOVEMENT AND WEEKLY FEEDINGS OF NEWLY HATCHED BRINE SHRIMP IN THE EVENING WHEN THEIR TENTACLES ARE BARED. THEY OCCUR IN MANY COLORS, BUT THE PURPLE VARIETY SEEMS TO BE AVAILABLE MOST OF THE TIME.

DENTED BROWN BRAIN, *SYMPHYLLIA RECTA*, DANA, 1846. A COMMON SPECIES OF THE MALDIVE ISLANDS, THIS SPECIES IS ALSO FOUND IN GREY, GREEN AND RED BUT FOR SOME REASON ONLY THE BROWN IS EXPORTED. IT REQUIRES VERY MODEST WATER MOTION, 10 HOURS OF INTENSE FLUORESCENT LIGHTING AND OCCASIONAL FEEDINGS (WEEKLY) WITH FRESHLY HATCHED BRINE SHRIMP WHEN THE TENTACLES ARE EXTENDED, USUALLY AT NIGHT. COLONIES ARE BRAIN SHAPED (ROUNDED).

Photo by Walt Deas.

FLAT GREEN BRAIN, *LOBOPHYLLIA CORYMBOSA*, FORSKÅL, 1775. PREFERS LITTLE WATER MOVEMENT BUT SUBSTANTIAL LIGHTING OF FULL FLUORESCENTS 8-12 HOURS PER DAY. MAY BE FED NEWLY HATCHED BRINE SHRIMP IN THE EVENING WHEN THEIR TENTACLES ARE EXPOSED. THOUGH NOT AGGRESSIVE, THEY SHOULD BE PLANTED WITH LOTS OF GROWING SPACE. THIS IS A COMMON CORAL FOUND FROM EAST AFRICA TO THE RED SEA TO AUSTRALIA AND TAHITI.

FLAT BRAIN, ROOT, TOOTH, LOBO, OPEN BRAIN CORAL, *LOBOPHYLLIA HEMPRICHII*, EHRENBERG, 1834. A VERY COMMON CORAL WHICH REQUIRES LOW WATER MOVEMENT AND HEAVY LIGHTING. THEY OFTEN ACCLIMATE TO LOWER LIGHTING, BUT 8 HOURS OF FULL FLUORESCENT LIGHTING IS STANDARD FOR THIS VERY COMMON SPECIES. MAY BE FED WEEKLY WITH NEWLY HATCHED BRINE SHRIMP WHEN TENTACLES ARE EXTENDED AT NIGHT. THEY ARE NOT FAST GROWING BUT SHOULD BE ISOLATED FROM DIRECT CONTACT WITH NEIGHBORS.

Photo by Walt Deas.

Photo by Walt Deas.

FLAT RED BRAIN, LOBO, ROOT, OPEN BRAIN CORAL, *LOBOPHYLLIA* SPECIES. THERE ARE MANY *LOBOPHYLLIA* VARIETIES WHICH HAVE NOT AS YET BEEN IDENTIFIED SCIENTIFICALLY. THIS SPECIES APPEARS FROM TIME TO TIME FROM THE MALDIVE ISLANDS. IT THRIVES ON LOW WATER MOVEMENT, HIGH LIGHTING WITH 8-10 HOURS OF INTENSE FLUORESCENT LIGHTING DAILY AND WEEKLY FEEDINGS OF NEWLY HATCHED BRINE SHRIMP WHEN THEIR TENTACLES ARE EXTENDED AT NIGHT.

MOTTLED FLAT BRAIN, LOBO, TOOTH, OPEN BRAIN CORAL, *LOBOPHYLLIA PACHYSEPTA*, CHEVALIER, 1975. A POPULAR SPECIES FOUND IN THE MALDIVE ISLANDS AND AROUND AUSTRALIA. IT DOES NOT LIKE HEAVY WATER MOVEMENT AND THRIVES ON LIGHT WATER MOVEMENT, PREFERABLY SURGES, LIKE WAVE-ACTION. IT NEEDS STRONG LIGHTING WITH FULL FLUORESCENT COVERAGE AT LEAST 10 HOURS PER DAY...12 HOURS IS EVEN BETTER IF THE CORALS ARE LOCATED DEEP IN YOUR MINI-REEF TANK. FEEDINGS ARE APPRECIATED.

BRAIN CORAL,
STAR CORAL,
BOULDER CORAL

THE GENUS *MONTASTREA*

This genus was constructed by de Blainville in 1830 based upon a description of *Astraea guettardi* described by Defrance in 1826. It has an old fossil record of 150 million years or more. There are about a dozen species but eventually there will probably only be half that amount as more observations are made in the mini-reef aquarium. The description of the genus is poor and very difficult to work with, but coral scientists and hobbyists easily recognize *Montastrea* by their extratentacular budding. (*Extratentacular budding* is when small polyps develop from adult polyps.)

BOULDER CORAL,
BRAIN CORAL,
STAR CORAL

MONTASTREA MAGNISTELLATA
Chevalier, 1971

(usually further identified by color)

This species is widely distributed from Indonesia south to Australia where it is found on

MONTASTREA MAGNISTELLATA, THE BOULDER OR BRAIN CORAL, IS IDEAL FOR THE BEGINNING MINI-REEFER. LIGHTING IS ACCEPTABLE AT LOW TO HIGH LEVELS; MODERATE WATER MOVEMENT AND LACK OF AGGRESSIVE GROWTH MAKES THIS THE IDEAL CANDIDATE AS A FIRST CORAL.

Photos by Walt Deas.

both coasts, including the Great Barrier Reef. It further extends through the Coral Sea to many isolated reefs in the South Pacific.

This species is an aquarium favorite because it is so colorful. Each specimen usually has 3-7 colors visible, though all the polyps on a given specimen are usually similarly pigmented. This is a shy species which does not do well with aggressively growing corals. Even in nature it is nowhere plentiful when in the company of other corals. The shapes of the polyps vary from individual to individual as well as within each colony. Once you study this coral you'll always be able to identify it even if the color is different.

They don't require feeding if they are kept with fishes in the mini-reef aquarium. They have nasty stinging tentacles, especially dangerous when they are handled at night or when the coral polyps are extended, so handle them carefully with heavy gloves.

They are easily split into pieces about 4 inches in diameter for reproductive purposes.

MONTASTREA SPECIES, THE PINK BRAIN CORAL, FROM MALAYSIA, IS A NEW ARRIVAL ON THE MINI-REEF SCENE. IT IS NOT VERY TOLERANT OF THE ERRORS COMMON TO MINI-REEFERS AND CAN ADJUST TO MOST LIGHT LEVELS. WATER SHOULD HAVE MODEST MOVEMENT AND ITS SLOW GROWTH IS COMMENDABLE.

Photos by Dr. Elizabeth M. Wood.

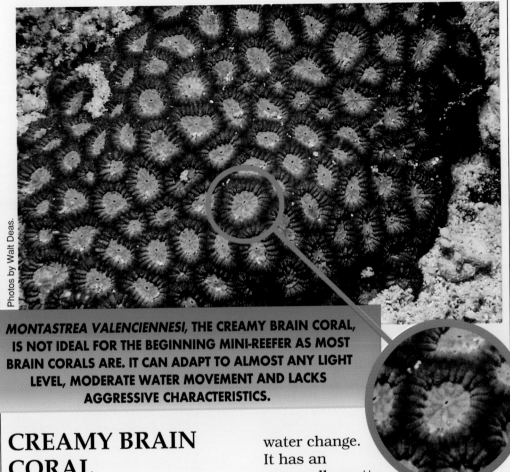

Photos by Walt Deas.

MONTASTREA VALENCIENNESI, THE CREAMY BRAIN CORAL, IS NOT IDEAL FOR THE BEGINNING MINI-REEFER AS MOST BRAIN CORALS ARE. IT CAN ADAPT TO ALMOST ANY LIGHT LEVEL, MODERATE WATER MOVEMENT AND LACKS AGGRESSIVE CHARACTERISTICS.

CREAMY BRAIN CORAL

MONTASTREA VALENCIENNESI
Edwards & Haime, 1848

This widely scattered species is found from Madagascar across the South Pacific to Australia, the Marshall Islands and the Coral Sea. It is rare in the hobby but aquaculturally raised specimens are available from time to time. Biologically it is a survivor and readily adapts to reef conditions. It is very hardy in the mini-reef aquarium as well. I have never seen more than isolated specimens. When I attempted to bring them home, they succumbed for lack of oxygen as sometimes it took weeks to get a water change.

It has an unusually pretty color pattern with its cream septa (the radial parts of the corallite inside the wall of the corallite) framing its green oral discs.

It rarely does well in the mini-reef aquarium even if it has room to grow. This is a fast growing species that requires supplemental feeding if there aren't enough fishes in the mini-reef aquarium with it. Baby brine shrimp are great food for all corals and all marine fishes, too.

Be careful of the septa, which are really sharp teeth, as they cut your skin easily. Always treat ALL cuts from corals.

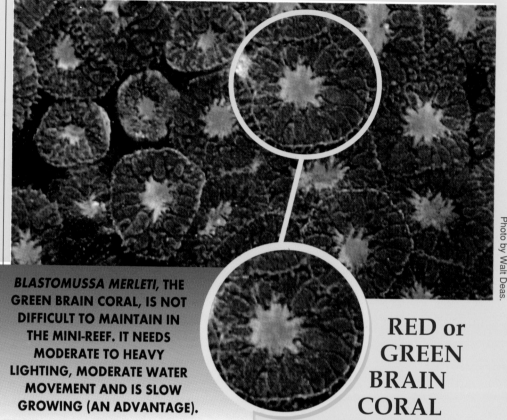

Photo by Walt Deas.

BLASTOMUSSA MERLETI, THE GREEN BRAIN CORAL, IS NOT DIFFICULT TO MAINTAIN IN THE MINI-REEF. IT NEEDS MODERATE TO HEAVY LIGHTING, MODERATE WATER MOVEMENT AND IS SLOW GROWING (AN ADVANTAGE).

RED or GREEN BRAIN CORAL

BLASTOMUSSA MERLETI
Wells,1961

SWOLLEN BRAIN CORAL, RED BRAIN CORAL, BURNING MOON CORAL

THE GENUS *BLASTOMUSSA*

The genus *Blastomussa* was described by Wells in 1961 with the description of the Australian species *Blastomussa merleti* Wells 1961. It is a small genus with only three species. The polyps are extended for night feeding only. The known species have several color morphs all of which favor red, but there is also a khaki green-brown.

The name derives from the Greek *blasto* meaning bud; *mussa* is a coral genus.

This well distributed species is found from the Great Barrier Reef of Australia to the large island of Madagascar. It occurs on both coasts of Australia up into New Caledonia. It is nowhere abundant and specimens in the aquarium trade are probably grown from fragments.

This coral is imperfectly dispersed over the surface of the colony. So much so, that it looks as if the polyps had been injured or destroyed and were growing back. This loss of symmetry is disturbing to most mini-reef aquarists who think their corals are diseased.

They like strong light and do not require feeding if they are housed with aquarium fishes.

Photo by Dr. Gerald R. Allen & Roger Steene; computer enhancement by Jan Balon

BLASTOMUSSA WELLSI, THE RED BRAIN CORAL, IS NOT DIFFICULT TO MAINTAIN WITH MODERATE LIGHTING AND WATER MOVEMENT. IT IS NON-AGGRESSIVE IN THE MINI-REEF AQUARIUM.

RED or GREEN BRAIN CORAL

BLASTOMUSSA WELLSI
Wijsman-Best, 1973

This is a lovely specimen, especially the red morph, which almost looks like it is made of soft velvet. The large polyps can cover the entire colony disguising the hard bases. It is as delicate as it looks and should not be subjected to very strong light, hot spots or strong currents. It thrives in the mini-reef if it is carefully placed and delicately handled.

Feeding is not necessary if kept with aquarium fishes, but a weekly feeding during the night is appreciated. The thick mantles are extended during the day, covering the structure of the colony. The polyps are extended only at night, which is why they should only be fed at night.

Photos by Walt Deas.

TRACHYPHYLLIA GEOFFROYI, THE GREEN OPEN BRAIN CORAL, IS FOR MINI-REEFERS WITH A LITTLE EXPERIENCE, THOUGH MANY BEGINNERS ACCLIMATE THEM WITHOUT ANY APPARENT DIFFICULTY. THEY REQUIRE MEDIUM LIGHTING, MODERATE WATER MOVEMENT AND THEY GROW SLOWLY AS DO ALL BRAIN CORALS.

OPEN BRAIN CORAL, ROUGH LEAF CORAL

THE GENUS *TRACHYPHYLLIA*
Edwards & Haime, 1848

This very small genus of one or two species is to be found around large, civilized, inhabited islands in the tropical seas. It is hugely abundant on the peaceful side of bays inside reefs. The name *Trachyphyllia* derives from *trachys* which means *rough* in Greek and *phyllon* which means *leaf* in Greek, thus *rough leaf*.

GREEN or RED OPEN BRAIN CORAL

TRACHYPHYLLIA GEOFFROYI
Audouin, 1826

This species occurs in two color morphs, one red and one green, a not unusual combination. They are easily collected because they reproduce sexually and the young usually attach to a dead, broken piece of coral or an unoccupied

Photo by Walt Deas.

The Green Open Brain Coral grows isolated and is easily collected for the mini-reef.

mollusk shell. When they outgrow this base, they fall loose and live in the sand or mud in lagoons. While possessing basically two color morphs, additional colors have been found, thus generating new species designation, but more thorough studies have indicated but a single species.

Photo by Walt Deas.

*Above: **Trachyphyllia geoffroyi**, the Green Open Brain Coral with polyps extended.* Below: **The Green Open Brain Coral showing a close-up of its mouth.**

Photo by Walt Deas.

Photo by Walt Deas.

Trachyphyllia geoffroyi, the Green Open Brain Coral, in its typical habitat.

The typically heavy base upon which the coral grows is indicative of a solitary coral piece imbedded in a soft medium. These are not corals for the beginner.

The artificial sea water used is very important as *geoffroyi* requires certain trace elements in its environment or in its diet. These trace elements seem to determine its color. When sufficient iodine is present, the color is usually reddish. Iron deficiency seems to make the coral green.

Huge quantities of this lovely coral are shipped from Malaysia, but they require a month of professional care before they are fit for the mini-reef aquarium. Their skeleton is typically shaped like a dog bone, with a knob on each end and a shank in the middle.

PINEAPPLE CORAL, CLOSED BRAIN CORAL

THE GENUS *PLATYGYRA*

This genus was constructed in 1834 by Ehrenberg from a specimen found in the Red Sea. It is often misnamed *Coeloria* Edwards & Haime 1843 and is well represented on reefs all around the world via some 30 species, most of which are synonyms. These corals are very difficult to distinguish, one from the other, and they exist on all sides and depths of major coral reef margins.

Platygyra was formed from the Greek words *platys* meaning *flat* and *gyros* meaning *wide*, probably referring to the wide, flat channels characteristic of these corals.

Photos by Walt Deas, Dr. Gerald R. Allen and Roger Steene.

PLATYGYRA LAMELLINA, **THE BROWN PINEAPPLE CORAL, IS SUITABLE FOR THE MINI-REEFER WITH A LARGE TANK OF 50 GALLONS OR MORE. IT HAS MODERATE LIGHTING REQUIREMENTS, MODERATE WATER MOVEMENT NEEDS AND IS NOT TOO AGGRESSIVE.**

BROWN or GREEN CLOSED BRAIN or PINEAPPLE CORAL

PLATYGYRA DAEDALEA
Ellis & Solander, 1786

This is easily the most common species of the genus. Large quantities are shipped into the aquarium trade from Malaysia and Singapore. They are very common on Malaysian reefs but are also found in quantity from the Red Sea eastward to Australia and the Marshall Islands. These colonies can be huge.

In the aquarium they form round, isolated pineapple-shaped colonies with varying colors. They usually have white either in the valleys or on the ridges. They do not require feeding if they are maintained in the mini-reef aquarium with fishes, but a monthly feeding of baby brine shrimp, at night when the tentacles are extended, seems to make them grow faster.

Photos by Walt Deas.

PLATYGYRA DAEDALEA, THE BROWN CLOSED BRAIN OR PINEAPPLE CORAL, REQUIRES MODERATELY HEAVY LIGHT, MODERATE WATER MOVEMENT AND IS SLIGHTLY AGGRESSIVE, WHICH MEANS IT SHOULD HAVE SOME ROOM FROM ITS CORAL NEIGHBORS. THE TWO PHOTOS SHOW THE DIFFERING STRUCTURE OF THE SURFACE OF *PLATYGYRA DAEDALEA.*

PLATYGYRA PINI, THE PURPLE OR BROWN PINEAPPLE OR CLOSED BRAIN CORAL, REQUIRES MODERATE LIGHT AND WATER MOVEMENT AND IS SLIGHTLY AGGRESSIVE.

Photos by Walt Deas.

PLATYGYRA *SINENSIS*, THE CHINESE CLOSED BRAIN CORAL, IS MAINTAINED IN THE MINI-REEF AQUARIUM WITH MODERATE LIGHTING, LOW WATER MOVEMENT AND A LITTLE SPACE BETWEEN ALL FLOWER ANIMALS.

Photos by Walt Deas.

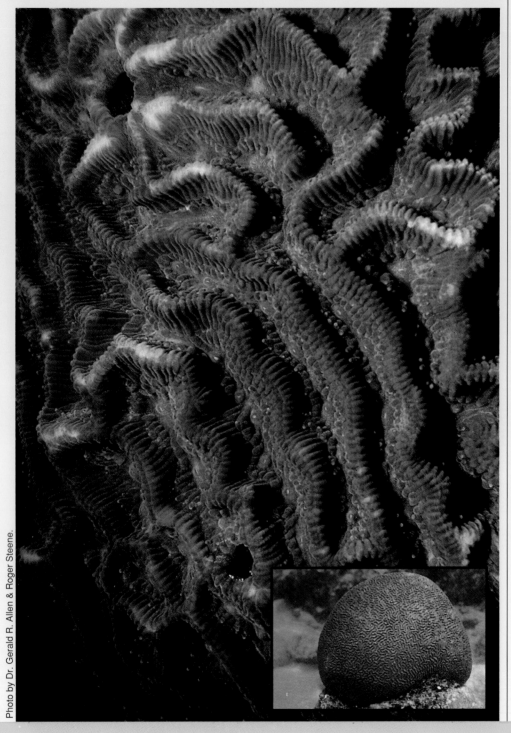

Photo by Dr. Gerald R. Allen & Roger Steene.

PLATYGYRA RYUKYUENSIS, THE JAPANESE CLOSED BRAIN CORAL, CAN BE MAINTAINED IN MINI-REEF TANKS THAT STAY BELOW 80°F. THEY NEED MODERATE AERATION, MEDIUM LIGHTING LEVELS AND ARE NOT AGGRESSIVE AT ALL. PHOTO BY WALT DEAS. THE INSERT SHOWS THE ENTIRE ANIMAL

TRUE-LEAF CORALS, ANCHOR CORALS, GRAPE CORALS

THE GENUS *EUPHYLLIA*

This genus was originally described by Dana in 1846. The meaning of the name *Euphyllia*, from the Greek, is *Eu* meaning *true*; *phyllon* meaning *leaf*. Probably referring to the impressive septa. There are about 16 species well distributed around the usual coral islands and atolls.

This genus is a natural for aquarists. For hundreds of years scientists relied upon the bleached skeleton of a coral to describe it and identify it. That doesn't work with *Euphyllia*. In order to identify these corals, you must study the polyps. This isn't too difficult because the polyps and tentacle are large and interestingly shaped. No one has proposed a theory for why these closely related corals have such different shapes. The hobby has attached names to the *Euphyllia* by their resemblance of the polyps to common items like grapes, anchors, hammers, torches and frogspawn.

Euphyllia are not hermaphroditic, that is, each animal has a separate sex, either male OR female. They release their sperm or eggs into the surrounding waters awaiting destiny for them to meet for purposes of external fertilization and reproduction. This type of reproduction assures the species of a wide and expanding distribution. *Euphyllia* have powerful stinging cells, if they have them at all. They also rely on sticky mucus and tiny hairs to capture the food and bring it into the oral disc.

ANCHOR CORAL, HAMMERHEAD CORAL

EUPHYLLIA ANCORA
Veron & Pichon, 1980

This species has a wide range from Australia's coasts, to Malaysia to Japan. Its tentacles are always extended during daylight hours and are so voluminous that it hides the skeletal base underneath. When the polyps retract, the septa are visible. The skeleton of this species is identical to the skeleton of *Euphyllia divisa* but the polyps are different. The color of this species varies from grey to orange with a green outer ridge.

In the mini-reef aquarium it does best in lower light and in water that barely moves. Feeding is not required if the mini-reef also houses fishes.

The polyps of *ancora* are beautifully distinctive, thus making this coral species extremely desirable. Luckily it is widely dispersed and easily propagated.

Photo by Dr. Gerald R. Allen, Roger Steene and Dr. Elizabeth M. Wood.

EUPHYLLIA ANCORA, THE ANCHOR CORAL, IS VERY EASY TO MAINTAIN PROVIDING TRACE ELEMENTS ARE REPLACED REGULARLY. THIS MEANS A 25% WATER CHANGE EVERY FEW WEEKS. THEY NEED MODERATE TO HEAVY LIGHTING AND NORMAL WATER MOVEMENT VIA A CANISTER FILTER. THEY ARE VERY AGGRESSIVE AS THEY EXTEND EXPLORATORY POLYP FINGERS.

FROGSPAWN CORAL

EUPHYLLIA DIVISA
Veron & Pichon, 1980

It is extremely difficult, if not impossible, to distinguish this species from *ancora* except by the shape of its polyps. When this coral is viewed in its natural habitat, it looks like the eggs of a large fish or frog (thus the name *frogspawn*). Its magnificence is enhanced by the fact that the polyps extend 24 hours a day unless they are disturbed or alarmed by physical or chemical stimuli. Large quantities of this species are exported from the Philippines, often under the sub-generic name *Fimbriaphyllia*. I have seen colonies as large as a yard across. They are very conspicuous in their habitat which is usually very shallow, muddy swamps and lagoons. In the aquarium they are best set into the fine sand with lots of room as they grow very quickly if given extremely bright light and supplementary food in the form of newly hatched brine shrimps. Their heavy base enables them to stay in position even when the tides or currents are fairly strong.

Color varieties of *divisa* are infinite, manifesting all shades of brown, green, pink, and grey with lighter polyp tips as contrasts.

EUPHYLLIA DIVISA, THE FROGSPAWN CORAL, IS NAMED AFTER THE TYPICAL MASS OF FROG'S EGGS WHICH SYMBOLIZES THE RADIANT TIPS OF THE POLYPS. THE POLYPS ARE DIVIDED BY THE EXTENDED CALICES. EASILY MANAGED WITH MODERATE TO HEAVY LIGHTING, MODERATE WATER MOVEMENT AND LOTS OF ROOM BETWEEN ITSELF AND ITS NEIGHBORING CORALS. PHOTO BY WALT DEAS.

TORCH CORAL,
POM-PON CORAL,
GRAPE CORAL

EUPHYLLIA GLABRESCENS
Chamisso & Eysenhardt, 1821

This species is as widespread as the entire genus from the South China Sea to the Red Sea to the Coral Sea to all coral-bearing areas in Australia. The colors can be sensational in their purity. Greens with white tentacular tips compete in the beauty contest with blues, greys and all colors in between. I started to keep a chart of the different colors and the ranges in which they occurred but it was inconclusive. It seems that fertilized eggs, being free floating, eventually attach to pieces of Sargassum weed and they are carried all through the tropical marine zone.

So while each location has only a single colored colony of *glabrescens*, you can't tell the origin of the specimen at hand.

None of the *Euphyllia* must be fed if they are kept with fishes in the mini-reef aquarium. Being so low in the aquarium they are showered with food in the form of fish feces and fish food debris. They do not have stinging tentacles so they are simple to handle, but this must be kept in mind when feeding them. Only use newly hatched brine shrimp, if any additional food is necessary (which it rarely is!).

Their branched base enables them to be secure in a wide variety of habitats, both in the mini-reef aquarium and in their normal range. Because they are almost always in an expanded condition, they are very easy to locate in their natural habitat and make excellent additions to the mini-reef tank.

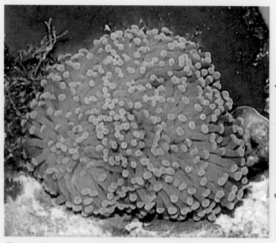

Euphyllia glabrescens.

Photo by Dr. Gerald R. Allen & Roger Steene.

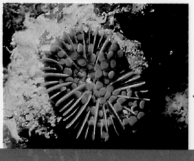

Photo by Walt Deas.

EUPHYLLIA SPECIES. REQUIRES MODEST TO HEAVY LIGHTING, SLOWLY MOVING WATER AND NO NEIGHBORS AS THIS IS AN AGGRESSIVE SPECIES.

EUPHYLLIA GLABRESCENS, THE TORCH CORAL, REQUIRES MODERATE TO HEAVY LIGHTING, MODERATELY MOVING WATER AND SEPARATION FROM OTHER CORAL ANIMALS. PHOTO BY WALT DEAS.

GRAPE CORAL,
FROGSPAWN CORAL

EUPHYLLIA CRISTATA
Chevalier, 1971

This species was originally described from New Caledonia where it is still very uncommon. Because it stays extended most of the time, though, it is so obvious that it lingers in your memory as being very prolific. Thus far it has only been found in Australia on both coasts and in New Caledonia, but it is being raised in aquaculture because of the high demand and the high mortality. This is truly a difficult coral to maintain because they are almost always traumatized during shipment.

When purchasing a specimen of *cristata*, examine it carefully. It must really look like a bunch of grapes without bald spots. Look at the elongated septa and be sure they are not broken. The septa should be easily visible between the tentacles. This species has no stinging cells so it is safe to handle, but the septa can be sharp and dangerous.

The branched base makes it easy to locate in the aquarium. It can be made comfortable at any level that received enough light. I have had the best success with all *Euphyllia* by keeping them on the sandy bottom, isolated, but with plenty of light. They never need feeding if there are fishes in the same mini-reef aquarium. They occur in shades of green with flesh-colored tips to the tentacles. The flesh colors vary greatly from skin pink to milk cream to yellow pink.

EUPHYLLIA CRISTATA, THE GRAPE OR FROGSPAWN CORAL, IS SLIGHTLY MORE DIFFICULT TO MAINTAIN THAN THE OTHER KNOWN *EUPHYLLIA* SPECIES BUT IF YOU HAVE KEPT OTHERS THEN TRY THIS ONE, TOO. IT NEEDS A MODERATE WATER CURRENT, 8 HOURS OF STRONG LIGHT PER DAY AND CANNOT TOLERATE TOUCHING ANOTHER CORAL. PHOTO BY U. ERICH FRIESE.

BUBBLE CORAL, PEARL CORAL, FULL CIRCLE CORAL, BALLOON CORAL

THE GENUS *PLEROGYRA*
Milne-Edwards & Haime, 1848

The genus name *Plerogyra* derives from the Greek *pleres* which means *full* and *gyros* which means *circle*. This is the basis for the common name which, though best suited, is hardly used in the English language. Bubble is the most widely used adjective describing the corals in the genus Plerogyra.

Plerogyra construct round colonies from large corallites which are usually 2 inches high with plenty of room between them. They form solidly packed surfaces when fully expanded and healthy. Their sexual reproduction results in single specimens (coralla) of juveniles strewn all around their habitat.

The vesicles disguise the skeleton of the coral, but they shrink at night when the tentacles become extended. The vesicles are usually round, thus the common names *bubble, full circle, pearl* and *balloon*. They measure more than half inch in diameter and are not uniform (different size vesicles on each animal). The septa look like the petals of a flower. They are not sharp, but the coral animal is still not safe to handle. While there are no stinging cells (nematocysts) on the bubbles, they are plentiful on the tentacles...and they really sting! I had burn marks on my arms for weeks as a result of handling *Plerogyra* I found in Singapore in 1955! Because they have the same arrangement of the corallites and colony shape as the genus *Euphyllia* they are usually confused by amateurs and dealers. But by closely studying the tentacles and vesicles, differentiation is simple. The septa of *Plerogyra* are also much more flowery and more widely separated.

BUBBLE CORAL, BLADDER CORAL, BALLOON CORAL, GRAPE CORAL

PLEROGYRA SINUOSA
Dana, 1846

A widely scattered species found from the Red Sea down the east coast of Africa across to the top half of Australia, north to Taiwan and some of the southern Japanese islands, as far east as Samoa and the Marshall Islands. Because of this distribution and their beautiful shape, this species is widely available. There are probably more than the six "species" mentioned in the literature because of the differing colors and shapes of the bubbles. The colors vary from grey to white to green to pink. A close look at

PLEROGYRA SINUOSA, THE BUBBLE CORAL, IS A BEAUTIFUL AND VERY EASY CORAL FOR BEGINNERS. IT REQUIRES MODERATE LIGHTING, MODERATE WATER MOTION AND LOTS OF SPACE BETWEEN IT AND THE NEXT CORAL ANIMAL. PHOTOS BY WALT DEAS.

the grapes disclose a surface which is wrinkled and differs from one another like fingerprints. Care must be taken not to injure those tentacles which have grapes; very powerful stinging tentacles protect them in nature from inquisitive fishes.

They thrive in the mini-reef with almost any kind of lighting providing it is intense. Their water should be barely moving for if it is too strong it might injure the vesicles. It is best planted away from other corals because of the strong stinging tentacles and the aggressive nature of its growth.

They thrive on brine shrimp even if they are housed in the mini-reef aquarium with fishes.

All species of *Plerogyra* require the same care in the mini-reef aquarium. They are all dangerous to handle due to their strong nematocysts (stingers).

AIR BUBBLE CORAL, PEARL CORAL, OCTOBUBBLE CORAL

THE GENUS *PHYSOGYRA*
Quelch, 1884

The name *Physogyra* derives from the Greek *physa* meaning *air bubble* and *gyros* meaning *circle*. In its natural habitat it can form a huge, rounded colony which is usually tan in color. There are three species and all are very dangerous because of their stinging capabilities. The skeleton looks like a series of thin disks. They are erratic in terms of the times of appearance of the extended vesicles. Their tentacles never completely retract. The *Physogyra* from the southern hemisphere appear fully extended during the day with stinging elongated tentacles at night. The opposite is true for the northern habitats.

PHYSOGYRA LICHTENSTEINI, THE PEARL CORAL, REQUIRES MODERATE LIGHTING AND WATER MOTION, AND PLENTY OF GROWING ROOM AS IT KILLS NEIGHBORING CORAL ANIMALS.

Photo by Dr. Elizabeth M. Wood.

PEARL CORAL,
BUBBLE CORAL,
GRAPE CORAL

PHYSOGYRA LICHTENSTEINI
Milne-Edwards & Haime, 1851

This species has a wide distribution from Madagascar to both coasts of Australia to the Marshall Islands. During the day the Australian race is completely covered with masses of vesicles which look exactly like a tight bunch of grapes. The polyps are extended only in the dark. These vesicles are very sensitive and retract quickly when disturbed.

They do well in the mini-reef aquarium and are found in varying colors from green to pink to grey. They are never easy to care for, but once they adjust, they grow very well. They like turbid conditions in nature and rely on the tidal currents to bring them food. They can be fed on newly hatched brine shrimp to make them grow faster. This species is often confused with the *Plerogyra*.

GALAXY CORAL,
MOON CORAL,
STAR CORAL

THE GENUS *GALAXEA*
Oken, 1815

The scientific name *Galaxea* derives from the Greek word *galaxaios* which means *milky*. There are a few dozen species and they have a wide range from East Africa to the Red Sea to the South China seas to Japan, south to cover all of tropical Australia and then as far east as the Marquesas. The colonies are round, solid and obvious. They are not as large as other solitary coral colonies. The tentacles are usually extended during the day and almost reach a half inch in length. This is an easy coral genus to identify as they don't look like anything else. In their usual habitat they are found in varied waters at varying depth. This ability to adapt makes them plentiful over their range and ideal for the home aquarium.

Photo by Walt Deas.

GALAXEA ASTREATA, THE MOON CORAL, REQUIRES SOME SKILL AND EXPERIENCE AND IS NOT RECOMMENDED FOR BEGINNERS. IT NEEDS SUBSTANTIAL LIGHTING, MODERATE WATER MOTION AND EXTENSIVE SEPARATION FROM ITS NEIGHBORS.

MOON, STAR,
GALAXY CORAL

GALAXEA ASTREATA
Lamarck, 1816

This species is widely distributed from the Red Sea to the South China Sea to the Fiji Islands and all around tropical

Photos by Walt Deas.

Galaxea astreata, the Moon Coral, clearly showing the coralites.

Australia. They are very common and plentiful. The colonies become extremely large. They are very aggressive. They do well in the mini-reef aquarium as long as they receive a minimum amount of bright light and some feedings with brine shrimp. I have found encrusting colonies wider across than I am tall (6 feet)! They do not like water which is too active so keep them from surges in your mini-reef.

They are easily recognized by the white tips of the polyps. They usually appear in green, brown, white, grey and pink.

Photo by Walt Deas.

GALAXEA FASCICULARIS, THE GALAXY CORAL, IS FOR THE ADVANCED MINI-REEFER. IT NEEDS A LOT OF LIGHT (10 HOURS OF 4-TUBE LIGHT PER DAY IN A 50 GALLON TANK), MODERATE WATER MOVEMENT AND SPACE SO ITS TENTACLES CANNOT REACH ITS NEIGHBORS.

GALAXY CORAL, GREEN STAR, MOON CORAL

GALAXEA FASCICULARIS
Linnaeus, 1767

This species has a very wide distribution from Fiji to China to the Red Sea, Australia and east to Samoa. It is an extremely attractive species because of its lack of symmetry. The corallites are of varying sizes up to 1/4 inch long. They have an abundant number of septa emanating from the middle of the corallite. Each polyp (the living part of the coral) can be imagined as a sea anemone and the colony can be imagined as a bouquet of flowers. There are many color varieties and the trade gives all of them different common names (such as Fluted Galaxy). They do best with supplemental feedings of baby brine shrimp and can be planted almost anywhere in the mini-reef aquarium where they receive quality light and calm water. They are not easy to keep alive and should not be the first coral species for the beginner.

GALAXEA SPECIES, THE GREEN STAR CORAL, IS EXTREMELY DIFFICULT TO MAINTAIN IN THE AVERAGE MINI-REEF AQUARIUM. IT REQUIRES MODERATE TO HEAVY LIGHT, MODERATE WATER MOTION AND LOTS OF ROOM. IT PROBABLY NEEDS A RARE TRACE ELEMENT FOR THEY LIVE FOR A FEW MONTHS AND THEN DIE. PHOTO BY WALT DEAS.

ABOVE: *FUNGIA SCUTARIA*, THE GREEN DISK, NEEDS 9 HOURS OF INTENSE LIGHT AND MODERATE WATER MOVEMENT. IT IS DANGEROUS TO OTHER CORALS IN WHICH IT HAS CONTACT. BELOW: A GROUP OF *FUNGIA* IN VARIOUS STAGES OF GROWTH.

Photos by Walt Deas.

MUSHROOM CORAL,
DISK CORAL,
CHINAMAN'S HAT

THE GENUS *FUNGIA*
Lamarck, 1801

The name *Fungia* derives from the Latin *fungus* which means *mushrooms*. This obviously describes the appearance of the colony. Specimens which have been injured during the growth period from juvenile to adult, are often malformed and may be very irregular in general shape. They vary tremendously in color showing the spectrum from tan through purple, pink, blue and green.

The septa are cyclical and uniform, forming a dome from the

Photo by U. Walt Deas.

FUNGIA SPECIES REQUIRE 8-10 HOURS OF STRONG LIGHT PER DAY, MODERATE WATER MOVEMENT AND SPACE BETWEEN IT AND ITS CORAL NEIGHBORS. THEY ARE THE MOST DIFFICULT CORALS THAT ARE RECOMMENDED FOR THE BEGINNING MINI-REEFER. THIS PHOTO SHOWS A GROUP OF DEVELOPING FUNGIA.

corallite. In nature small specimens are found near the colony. These small specimens are fastened to butts of dead coral or rocks. Usually these juveniles are less than 2 inches in their largest dimension. As they grow larger, as solitary animals, they eventually reach a diameter of two feet and become either round, flat or slightly domed. The mouth is very obvious in the middle of the center of the corallum to the perimeter. This is a very diverse group which has been further broken down into five subgenera. They have an almost unique ability to move by using the tentacles around the perimeter of the corallum. At least 20 species have been described from the Red Sea to the eastern coast of tropical Africa, through the South China Sea across all the coral atolls of the South Pacific, including northern Australia. Most, if not all, the *Fungia* are capable of dangerous stings to humans and adjacent coral neighbors as well. Tentacles are extended only at night. They are quickly retracted if disturbed...real *touch-me-nots*.

If a colony is destroyed say, for instance, by the propeller of a motor boat, almost every piece will

mistaken for *Fungia danai*. It is mostly brownish and usually variegated. It can be kept in any mini-reef aquarium and if a healthy juvenile specimen is obtained, they are easy to care for. Adult specimens are often a problem. Place them in the sand away from other living things and keep your eye on

Photo by Walt Deas.

FUNGIA FUNGITES, THE MUSHROOM OR FUNGUS CORAL, REQUIRES 8 HOURS OF GOOD LIGHT PER DAY, MODERATE WATER MOVEMENT AND SEPARATION FROM OTHER CORALS.

develop into a juvenile and eventually form their own colony. These are very adaptable animals.

FUNGUS,
MUSHROOM, DISK CORAL

FUNGIA FUNGITES
Linnaeus, 1758

This species is frequently

them as they will move if things are not to their liking. They detest strong water currents and poor light. If another corallum gets in their way when they are moving, they will usually attack it with their nematocysts.

They are everywhere common when they exist and are readily recognized by their pointed triangular teeth.

Photos by Walt Deas.

FUNGIA DANAI, THE PURPLE MUSHROOM CORAL, REQUIRES STRONG LIGHTING 8 HOURS PER DAY, MODERATE WATER MOVEMENT AND SEPARATION FROM NEIGHBORING CORALS.

FUNGUS,
MUSHROOM, DISK CORAL

FUNGIA DANAI
Milne-Edwards & Haime, 1851

This species is frequently mistaken for *Fungia fungites*. It has the same brownish colors and the same mottling. Specimens which have not been scientifically identified show up in the aquarium trade as purple (and are called Purple Disks). All *Fungia* species should be handled VERY carefully. Not only do they sting and cut, but they are easily damaged. Never handle them when they are inflated as you might rupture a vesicle. If you want to remove them to another min-reef aquarium, slide a soup plate under them and move them with the plate filled with water so the base doesn't dry or trap polluted air. They are hardy against marine pathogens but helpless when dealing with freshwater or airborne pathogens.

PLATE, GRAPE, DISK, MUSHROOM or LONG-TENTACLED CORAL

THE GENUS *HELIOFUNGIA*
Wells, 1966

The scientific name derives from Greek and Latin. *Helios* means *sun* and *fungus* means *mushroom*. The shape of the coral is round like the sun and the tentacles radiating from the center are like the rays of the sun. This genus only has one species, thus far, and was constructed after 130 years of debate, starting with Quoy & Gaimard in 1833. Based upon skeletons only, this genus is so close to *Fungia* that it was considered as a subgenus based upon *Fungia actiniformis* Quoy & Gaimard 1833. But when mini-reef aquarists kept them, the difference in the polyps was sufficient for Wells to establish them as a full genus in 1966.

HELIOFUNGIA ACTINIFORMIS, THE LONG-TENTACLED PLATE CORAL, REQUIRES MODERATE LIGHTING, A MODERATE WATER FLOW AND SEPARATION FROM ITS NEIGHBORS.

Photo by Walt Deas.

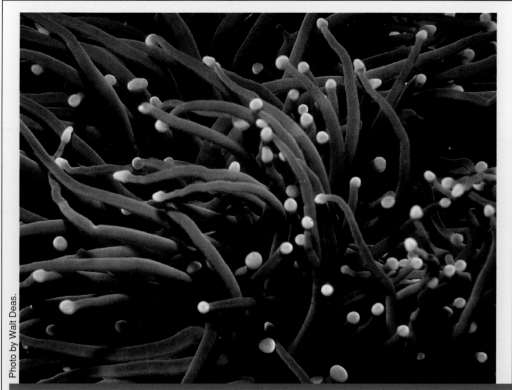

Photo by Walt Deas.

HELIOFUNGIA ACTINIFORMIS HAS LONG POLYPS AND TENTACLES, PERHAPS THE LONGEST OF ANY CORAL.

PLATE, GRAPE, DISK, MUSHROOM or LONG-TENTACLED CORAL

HELIOFUNGIA ACTINIFORMIS
Quoy & Gaimard 1833

(often further described by the color)

This is a solitary, non-colonizing, free-living coral which has the largest polyps of all corals. A single animal can be almost two feet in diameter and look like a sea anemone... except they don't have any fish nestling in them. These are weird corals. Their tentacles can range in color from green to purple to pink, but the ends are white. These white tips rub off very easily! It is very sticky too, assumedly to help in the food collecting function. They are not sensitive and rarely retract their tentacles unless they are ill or unhappy. The tentacles are guarded when retracted by very formidable teeth on the septa.

They range from northern Australia (including the barrier reef) to almost the southern islands of Japan. They are aggressive and not too difficult to care for. They can stand moderately moving water as they are normally found in shallow, flat sandy substrata in lagoons. They are very obvious because they are so large and solitary, often being the only coral in the immediate area.

Photos by Walt Deas.

ABOVE AND BELOW: TWO VIEWS OF *HELIOFUNGIA ACTINIFORMIS* SHOWING THE COLOR VARIATIONS WITHIN THE SAME ANIMAL.

FUNGIA SCRUPOSA REQUIRES THE SAME CARE AS FUNGIA DANAI. PHOTO BY WALT DEAS.

Photo by Dr. Elizabeth M. Wood.

HALOMITRA PILEUS, THE NEPTUNE'S CAP CORAL, HAS MODERATE LIGHTING NEEDS, MODERATE WATER FLOW AND IS NOT AGGRESSIVE AGAINST OTHER CORALS.

THE GENUS *HALOMITRA*
Dana, 1848

The *Halomitra* derives from the Greek *halos* meaning *sea* and *mitra* meaning *cap*, referring to the cap-like shape in which this coral is usually found.

NEPTUNE'S CAP,
DOME, HELMET, BONNET CORAL

HALOMITRA PILEUS
Linnaeus, 1758

This coral exists in a wide distribution from the eastern coast of Africa, Madagascar to the south China Sea, further north to the southern Japanese islands then south to the Great Barrier Reef then throughout many of the coral atolls of the South Pacific. The polyps are small and only extend during the night. The colors are extremely variable, though the basic color is brown, it has outlines of pink, green and purple.

It forms colonies on the sand or other soft substrata where it may grow to 2 feet in diameter. The mouth often is nicely colored in blue, grey, green or even yellow. There are 5 or 6 nominal species but probably only one that is valid.

In the mini-reef aquarium they are not easy to care for. They are slow growing and need strong light but only for 8 hours a day. They require moderately moving water to bring them nutrition from the fish's waste. A small feeding of newly hatched brine shrimp is appreciated.

Photo by Dr. Herbert R. Axelrod.

CATALAPHYLIA JARDINEI, THE ELEGANCE CORAL, IS A BEAUTIFUL CORAL FOR BEGINNERS. IT CAN TAKE MODERATE LIGHTING, A LIGHT WATER MOVEMENT AND IS NOT TOO AGGRESSIVE. IT IS IDEAL FOR THE BEGINNING MINI-REEFER.

THE GENUS *CATALAPHYLIA*
Wells, 1971

The scientific name derives from Dr. Rene *Catala* who researched marine subjects and ran a mini-reef public aquarium set on top of the ocean with running fresh sea water.

ELEGANCE,
CATALA'S CORAL

CATALAPHYLLIA JARDINEI
Saville-Kent, 1893

This is a truly magnificent coral. It is practically identical to *Euphyllia* and would not survive a modern analysis. Dr. Catala discovered that even though this is a very colorful species under natural light, when it is subjected to ultra-violet light only, the oral disk becomes bright green and the tentacles become bright blue with magenta tips. I saw three large aquaria in Catala's public aquarium, all with UV–light and fishes with night vision. This species was made for the aquarium and is one of the most simple species to maintain. It occurs in many colors over its tremendous range from the Seychelles off the eastern coast of Africa to the Great Barrier Reef, throughout the south China Seas north to southern Japan. Each locality might have a

Photo by Dr. Herbert R. Axelrod.

Left: The genus *Catalaphyllia* was named to honor Rene Catala of the Noumea Aquarium. He is shown here, left to right, with Pierre Laboute, Dr. Conde of the Nancy Aquarium, Rene Catala, Evelyn Axelrod and Mrs. Catala.

***CATALAPHYLLIA* SPECIES LOOKS AND ACTS LIKE A SEA ANEMONE. THIS ATTRACTS ANEMONEFISHES AS YOU CAN SEE IN THIS WONDERFUL PHOTO. THIS IS A VERY EASY SPECIES TO CARE FOR WITH MODERATE LIGHTING, WATER MOVEMENT AND SPACE.**

different color morph but the prettiest one comes from the South Pacific. They like to be stuck in the sand with plenty of room. Their lighting is not too demanding. Perhaps 4 hours of strong light per day. When they are happy, their tentacles are extended day and night as they search for food. They require some baby brine shrimp once a week. They usually destroy any corals which are adjacent to them. I have seen them grow to 18 inches across.

There is no need for strong aeration if the corals are fed.

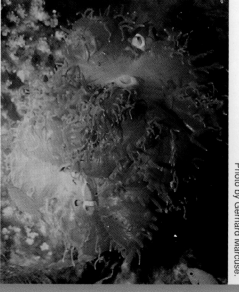

Photo by Gerhard Marcuse.

***CATALAPHYLLIA PLICATA*, THE GOLDEN ELEGANCE CORAL, IS A WONDERFUL CORAL FOR BEGINNERS. IT REQUIRES THE SAME CARE AS *C. JARDINEI*.**

Photo by Prof. C.W. Emmens.

CATALAPHYLLIA PLICTATA, THE GREEN ELEGANCE, IS SUITABLE FOR BEGINNING MINI-REEFERS. IT REQUIRES MODERATE LIGHTING AND WATER MOTION. IT NEEDS SPACE BETWEEN ITSELF AND ITS NEIGHBORS. PHOTO BY MP&C PIEDNOIR AQUA PRESS.

BRANCH, CABBAGE, CANDY, TRUMPET or TARGET (BULLSEYE) CORAL

THE GENUS *CAULASTREA*
Dana, 1846

The name of this genus derives from the Greek *kaulos* meaning *cabbage stalk* and *aster* meaning *star*. There are about 8 corals called *Caulastrea*, but only 4 are confirmed as true species. They range from East Africa, covering most of tropical Australia to Indonesia, Japan, Malaysia and as far east as Samoa.

WEST AUSTRALIAN CAULASTREA

***CAULASTREA TUMIDA*,**
Matthal, 1928

These corals are rare even though they range from Madagascar to Western Australia. They have small corallites about half inch in diameter. They are a boring color, usually grey. I have seen very few specimens on the Great Barrier Reef, but they are quite common along the sandy shores of Western Australia. They are easy to care for but not exciting in color. They thrive with low light, light feeding and a minimal water current.

CAULASTREA TUMIDA IS NOT A TYPICAL SPECIES OF THE GENUS *CAULASTREA*, BUT IT DOES WONDERFULLY WELL IN THE AQUARIUM WITH MODERATE LIGHTING AND A MODEST FLOW OF WATER. IT DOES NOT BOTHER OTHER CORALS. A GREAT SPECIES FOR BEGINNERS!

Photo by U. Erich Friese.

TRUMPET CORAL,
CANDY, BULLSEYE
CAULASTREA ECHINULATA
Edwards & Haime, 1849

The tentacles are normally retracted during the day. At night the polyps are so distended that they cover the whole animal and are extremely beautiful. They are easy to keep and are not a danger to other coral species. They do best with 8 hours of bright light per day and weekly feeding of baby brine shrimp. It relies upon water movement to bring its food to small tentacles.

a bunch of flowers held in your hand. Each stem has a beautiful polyp which look like peppermint candy with its characteristic stripes. They are found in browns, reds, greens and pink. They are easy to care for as are all the corals in this genus.

Photo by Dr. Elizabeth M. Wood.

CAULASTREA ECHINULATA, THE TRUMPET CORAL, IS EASY TO CARE FOR WITH MODERATE LIGHT AND WATER MOVEMENT. IT IS NOT AGGRESSIVE EITHER.

CANDYCANE,
BRANCH CORAL
CAULASTREA FURCATA
Dana, 1846

Colonies of this beauty are like

Photo by Dr. Elizabeth M. Wood.

CAULASTREA FURCATA, THE CANDYCANE, CAN ONLY BE POSITIVELY IDENTIFIED BY ITS SKELETON, AS SHOWN HERE. IT REQUIRES MODERATE WATER, MODERATE LIGHTING AND IS NOT AGGRESSIVE.

BRANCH CANDY CORAL
CAULASTREA CURVATA
Wijsman-Best, 1972

These are poorly arranged corallites with a diameter of 1/3 inch. The outside rim of the colony seems to have curved corallites. Only a light brown race is known thus far as they are fairly rare in their known range of the Coral Sea and the Great Barrier Reef. They are easy to care for so follow the instructions for the rest of the genus.

ELEPHANT NOSE

THE GENUS *MYCEDIUM*
Oken, 1815

This genus contains one species and derives its name from the Greek: *mykes* means knobbed like a mushroom; *-idion* makes the *mykes* diminutive (*small knobs*). it has mostly separate corallites and huge colonies larger than a man's height! The corallite diameters could be half an inch in diameter in such large colonies.

ELEPHANT NOSE

MYCEDIUM ELEPHANTOTUS
Pallas, 1766

This widely dispersed and very common coral is found in almost every ecological niche in which any coral is found (almost!). They change their 'skin' to fit the niche and, as a result, you get specimens with just about every type of septa and calice usually found amongst corals. It has been concluded that all of these variations are found in this one species. They do best in the aquarium if planted in the sand or amongst other corals as they are not usually aggressive. They are found in grey, brown, green or skin pink. Each animal, though, only shows one color. Their polyps are only extended at night and they do best if fed brine shrimp once a week. They depend on water movement to bring the food to their tentacles.

This species ranges from the Red Sea, down the east African coast to South Africa, then across Australia to 1,000 miles further east and then north to Japan.

MYCEDIUM ELEPHANTOTUS, THE ELEPHANT NOSE, REQUIRES MODERATE LIGHTING, MODERATE WATER FLOW AND IS NOT AGGRESSIVE, BUT IT IS NOT FOR BEGINNING MINI-REEFERS.

Photo by Walt Deas.

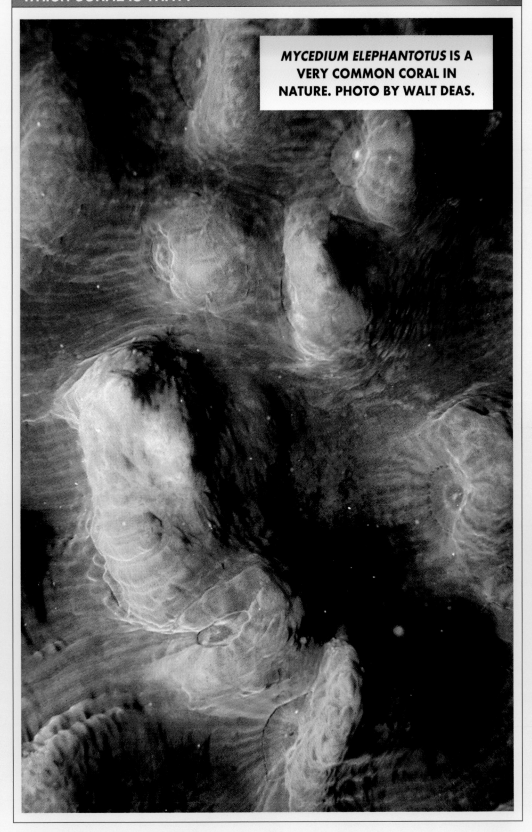

MYCEDIUM ELEPHANTOTUS IS A VERY COMMON CORAL IN NATURE. PHOTO BY WALT DEAS.

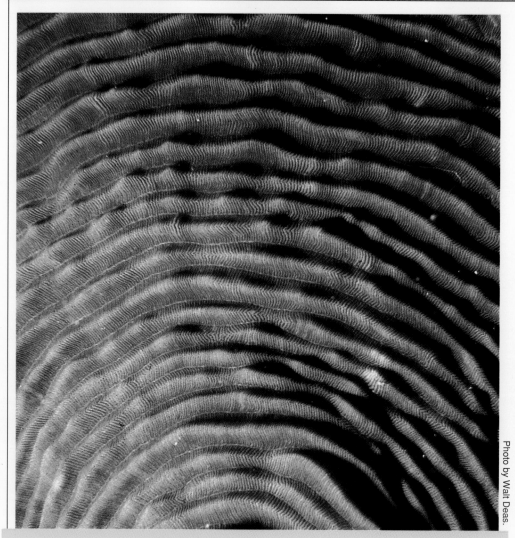

Photo by Wat Deas.

PACHYSERIS SPECIOSA, THE ELEPHANT SKIN OR SEA CACTUS, REQUIRES A SUBSTANTIAL WATER FLOW AND A LOT OF LIGHT. IT IS NOT AGGRESSIVE.

ELEPHANT SKIN

THE GENUS *PACHYSERIS*
Milne-Edwards & Haime, 1849

The name of this genus derives from the Greek *pachys* meaning *thick* and *seris* meaning *lettuce.* There are a dozen species in the literature, but only two species have been verified by modern systematists. They have a wide range from the Red Sea to South Africa, across Australia's northern coast to the Marquesas north to Malaysia, Sri Lanka and the Ryukyus. They are very easy to recognize in nature. They have a similar looking coral found in the West Indies called *Agaricia*. They are weird in the sense that their polyps are never extended, neither day nor night! While the literature mentions up to a dozen species, modern systematists agree that there are only two true species.

Photo by Walt Deas.

PACHYSERIS RUGOSA **IS RARE AND EXPENSIVE. IT IS FAIRLY DIFFICULT TO MAINTAIN BUT IT HAS THE SAME REQUIREMENTS AS** *P. SPECIOSA.*

SEA CACTUS,
ELEPHANT SKIN, PHOTOGRAPH, CORDUROY CACTUS

PACHYSERIS RUGOSA
Lamarck, 1801

This species is normally an unspectacular grey or brown. It becomes a huge colony if it has enough room in its natural habitat. It is not unusual to find groups 25 feet in width. They are very commonly found in turbid waters which are shallow. It requires a lot of light with lots of water action. Though pieces are sold for mini-reef aquariums, they are not really adaptable to such small surroundings.

PACHYSERIS SPECIOSA
Dana, 1846

This species is very similar to *rugosa* except for the columellae, the structure of the skeleton in the middle of the corallite. In nature it barely reaches 6 feet in diameter. It is the same brownish grey as *rugosa* and the two are frequently confused with each other. They do not require feeding if they have fishes living with them in the mini-reef aquarium, though they require a high quality artificial sea salt with the full range of trace elements.

Photo by Walt Deas.

CYNARINA LACRYMALIS, THE BUTTON CORAL, HAS MODEST LIGHTING REQUIREMENTS, MODEST WATER MOTION AND IS NOT AGGRESSIVE. THIS BEAUTY IS NICE FOR THE MORE AGGRESSIVE BEGINNING MINI-REEFER.

THE GENUS *CYNARINA*
Brueggemann, 1877

This is a popular genus for scientists and ten species are found in the literature. The name derives from the Greek word *kinara* which means artichoke; the *ina* means *similar to.* At the present time systematists only recognize one species which has a wide distribution from the Red Sea to Madagascar to Japan and the Fiji Islands. A second doubtful species is found only in the Red Sea but it was the type species described by Brueggemann in 1877 as *Cynarina savignyi.* In any case, both species require the same care.

BUTTON,
FLAT BRAIN,
DOUGHNUT

CYNARINA LACRYMALIS
Edwards & Haime, 1848

If there has to be a most beautiful coral, perhaps this one should be considered. The problem is that it occurs in so many colors, shapes and sizes, that it masquerades under many common and scientific names. In any case, it is easy to care for, requires very little feeding, moderate lighting about 6 hours per day, very gentle water movement and protection from aggressive corals. The translucent

Photo by Walt Deas.

Cynarina lacrymalis **occurs in many colors.**

body wall allows visions of the septa. Each specimen can easily be a different color. They change form at night when the huge lobes are withdrawn and the non-robust tentacles appear. Once the tentacles capture a baby brine shrimp, the tentacles bend towards the mouth to deliver the prey. They live anyplace in the mini-reef aquarium, either attached to a stony surface or planted in the sand.

THE GENUS *SCOLYMIA*
Haime, 1852

The name derives from the Greek meaning *artichoke*. In older literature, this genus was described as coming from the Atlantic Ocean and Caribbean Sea but further study by systematists indicate that it is a widespread genus of six valid, true species with representatives in the Caribbean (down to Brazil!), and the rest coming from the Indo-Pacific. It is

Photo by Dr. Patrick Colin.

***SCOLYMIA VITIENSE*, THE BROWN DOUGHNUT, MAY ALSO BE RED OR EVEN GREEN. IT HAS MODEST LIGHTING NEEDS, MODERATE WATER MOVEMENT AND IS NOT OVER AGGRESSIVE.**

***SCOLYMIA LACERA*, THE PURPLE DOUGHNUT, WAS PHOTOGRAPHED IN JAMAICA. IT IS THE EASIEST OF THE *SCOLYMIA* TO MAINTAIN AND HAS THE SAME REQUIREMENTS WITH MODERATE WATER MOVEMENT, MODERATE LIGHTING AND IS NON-AGGRESSIVE.**

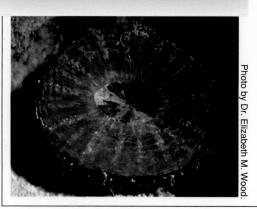

Photo by Dr. Elizabeth M. Wood.

found everywhere in Australia in which any coral is found. The polyps are only expanded at night.

RED DOUGHNUT, GREEN ARTICHOKE

SCOLYMIA VITIENSIS
Brueggemann, 1877

Based upon a specimen from Fiji, this species opened up a dramatic discussion of the distribution of corals. This species is found in temperate as well as tropical waters. As such it is found all around Australia and all the way north to Japan. While it

Photo by U. Erich Friese.

SCOLYMIA AUSTRALIS, THE DOUGHNUT, ARTICHOKE OR AUSTRALIAN SAUCER CORAL, IS A MINI-REEF FAVORITE WHICH APPEALS TO HOBBYISTS READY TO GRADUATE TO A SLIGHTLY MORE DIFFICULT FLOWER ANIMAL. IT HAS MODEST LIGHTING NEEDS, MODERATE WATER MOVEMENT AND IS NOT TOO AGGRESSIVE.

is everywhere rare, specimens are found in every coral area. The tentacles are extended at nighttime only. It only has a single polyp which may be red, but also may be green or brown. The green one is sold as *australis*. It comes from deep reefs and is very easily intimidated by other corals. So plant it with lots of room around it. The lighting requirements are minimal, though it requires moving waters. Studies have been done on its aggressive (or lack thereof) behavior. They

should be fed with newly hatched brine shrimp.

ARTICHOKE, DOUGHNUT

SCOLYMIA AUSTRALIS
Edwards & Haime, 1849

This is another solitary, single-polyp which is very colorful. It occurs in Australia in tropical and temperate waters and morphs occur in red, blue, green and sand. Care is the same as *vitiensis* and the juveniles of both species are almost indistinguishable.

CUP, BOWL, VASE CORAL

THE GENUS *TURBINARIA*
Oken, 1815

The name derives from the Latin word *turbinatus* which means *cone-shape*. It is the only genus of hermatypic, reef builders in the family Dendrophyllidae, and it grows very quickly in nature. It is hugely variable and is a challenge for all systematists. The literature describes 80 species which extend from the Red Sea to South Africa, most of tropical Australia to Japan and east to the Pitcairn Islands. Experiments have shown that the form of these corals change when their habitat changes. Deep water forms change to appear like shallow water forms and shallow water forms change to look like deep water forms. These corals breed in the fall when the water temperature begins to drop! They have distinct sexes. Except for *peltata*, the polyps are nocturnal.

BROWN CUP, VASE, PAGODA

TURBINARIA PELTATA
Esper, 1794

Large, daytime polyps make this an aquarium favorite, even

though the colors are far from exciting (brown or grey). They are abundant in their range and form large colonies up to 10 feet across. They are hardy and chunks are easily broken off for shipment to mini-reef aquarists because they heal so quickly. The retracted animal looks nothing like the expanded form. Though they grow fast they do not seem to

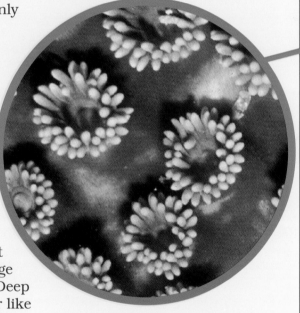

attack other species. Their shape is so variable that they are known under a dozen aliases (common names). In the aquarium they require 6 hours of bright lighting, weekly feeding of newly hatched brine shrimp, and lots of room. Water movement should be medium and they should be carefully observed when introduced to your mini-reef aquarium to be sure their wounds heal. Dying specimens should be discarded or transferred to a hospital tank away from other reef animals.

Photos by Walt Deas.

TURBINARIA PELTATA, THE CUP CORAL, PRESENTS SMALL PROBLEMS WHICH ARE EASILY SOLVED WITH MODERATE LIGHTING AND WATER MOTION AND ROOM TO GROW AS THEY ARE FAST GROWERS BUT DO NOT ATTACK NEIGHBORS.

OCTOPUS
TURBINARIA PATULA
Dana, 1846

The ends of the tentacles on this species are a dead giveaway. They look like the sucking disks of an *Octopus*. These corals need cool water about 65-70°F. They die in water which is too warm and for this reason they are not recommended for the mini-reef aquarium. They are never found in the tropics.

YELLOW CUP
TURBINARIA FRONDENS
Dana, 1846

Juveniles are small specimens are usually cup-shaped, but larger

TURBINARIA FRONDENS, THE YELLOW CUP CORAL, REQUIRES MODERATE LIGHTING AND SLIGHTLY LOWER TEMPERATURES ABOUT 78°F. MODERATE WATER MOVEMENT AND GROWING ROOM ARE REQUIRED FOR THIS FAST-GROWING SPECIES.

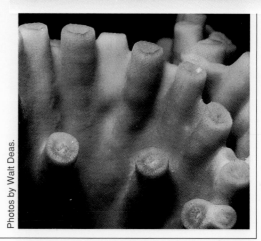

Photos by Walt Deas.

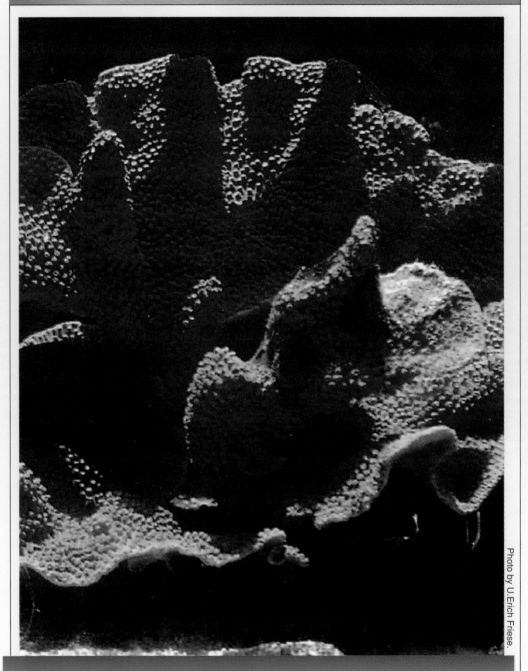

Photo by U.Erich Friese.

***TURBINARIA MESENTERINA,* THE PAGODA OR CUP CORAL, REQUIRES MODERATE WATER MOTION AND LIGHTING. IT REQUIRES GROWING SPACE.**

specimens in nature are often irregularly shaped. They prefer temperate waters but I have collected them in Thailand and Japan. They are very similar to *patula* and only skeletal differences separate the two species. Care same as for other members of the genus.

Photo by U. Erich Friese.

TURBINARIA RENIFORMIS, THE YELLOW SCROLL CORAL, REQUIRES MODERATE WATER MOTION, MODERATE LIGHTING AND SPACE TO GROW.

PAGODA,
CUP, BOWL, LETTUCE CORAL

TURBINARIA MESENTERINA
Lamarck, 1816

A proper colony of *mesenterina* looks like a head of lettuce, but, depending on the depth, can also take on other shapes and colors.

Generally they are brown to green but never brightly so. They grow well at any location in the aquarium. In their range, their choice of habitat varies from shallow to deep reef locations. Given high intensity light in 12 hour doses and their form changes from 4 hours of light. They are confused with *reniformis*.

YELLOW SCROLL,
YELLOW CUP,
YELLOW SCROLL

TURBINARIA RENIFORMIS
Bernard 1896

This lovely species closely resembles *mesenterina* especially when it grows in colonies in shallow waters. The temperate water form from southern Japan looks like flat mushrooms growing on a tree! They should be given intense lighting until they become established; watch them as they quickly pollute the water if they die in the mini-reef aquarium. They are found in shades of yellow and green with attractive, contrasting edges.

PIMPLE CUP
SPOTTED CORAL

TURBINARIA STELLULATA
Lamarck, 1816

This is a rare species which is the easiest of the *Turbinaria* to maintain in the mini-reef aquarium. In Australia I found them in clear, almost motionless water where they formed 3 feet wide colonies. I was able to ship them to Europe where they survived. They require some feeding and lots of light; perhaps 8 hours of intense light per day.

TURBINARIA SPECIES, THE PIZZA PIE, IS A RELATIVELY EASILY KEPT SPECIES WHICH REQUIRES MODERATE WATER MOVEMENT, MODERATE LIGHTING AND IS NOT AGGRESSIVE.

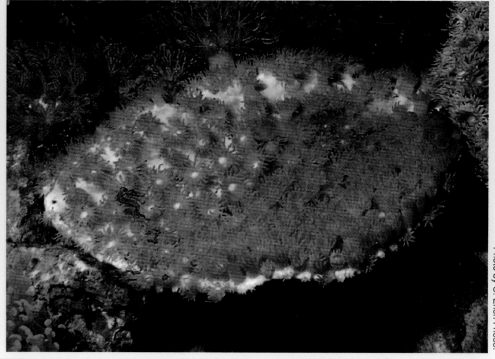

Photo by U. Erich Friese.

Photo by Dr. Elizabeth M. Wood.

TURBINARIA STELLULATA, THE PIMPLE CUP SPOTTED CORAL, IS THE EASIEST OF THE GENUS TO MAINTAIN IN YOUR MINI-REEF AQUARIUM. IT REQUIRES THE USUAL MODERATE WATER MOVEMENT AND LIGHTING AND IS USUALLY NON-AGGRESSIVE SO IT CAN BE LOCATED CLOSE TO OTHER FLOWER ANIMALS.

SCROLL CORAL

TURBINARIA BIFRONS
Brueggemann, 1877

These are rarely seen corals which are available in brown, green or grey. Their margins are contrasting and they prefer cooler waters about 68-70°F.

TURBINARIA CONSPICUA, THE LETTUCE CORAL, REQUIRES MODERATE WATER AND MODERATE LIGHTING. IT NEEDS GROWING SPACE.

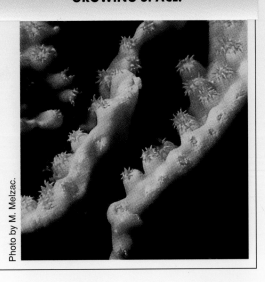

Photo by M. Melzac.

LETTUCE CORAL

TURBINARIA CONSPICUA
Bernard, 1896

This tannish coral in rarely seen in nature but it is increasingly being imported from Western Australia. It is confused with *bifrons* which has larger polyps. Care is the same as the other species except the temperature of the water should be about 76°F.

Photo by Dr. Elizabeth M. Wood.

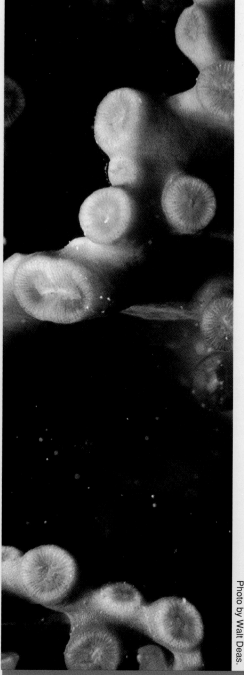

Photo by Walt Deas.

TURBINARIA RADICALIS, **THE ROOTED CORAL, REQUIRES TEMPERATE WATER ABOUT 72°F. MODERATE WATER MOVEMENT, MODERATE LIGHTING AND GROWING SPACE ARE ITS OTHER REQUIREMENTS. THIS IS A RARE SPECIES WITH A VERY BEAUTIFUL GOLDEN SHADE.**

ROOTED CORAL
TURBINARIA RADICALIS
Bernard 1896

Only found in temperate areas, this rare coral occurs in browns and greens. It seems to thrive when cared for as with the other temperate coral species in this genus.

YELLOW ROOTED CORAL
TURBINARIA HERONENSIS
Wells, 1958

The polyps of this rare species are a pretty shade of yellowish gold. It is only found in Australia where it is often kept in mini-reef aquariums. It requires a lot of light (10 hours a day) to maintain its colors, otherwise it fades. It thrives on weekly feeding of newly hatched brine shrimp.

TURBINARIA HERONENSIS, **THE YELLOW ROOTED CORAL, NEEDS MAXIMUM LIGHTING, MODERATE WATER MOVEMENT AND SUPPLEMENTAL FEEDING OF NEWLY HATCHED BRINE SHRIMP WEEKLY.**

Photo by Walt Deas.

ABOVE: *TURBINARIA BIFRONS*, THE AUSTRALIAN CUP CORAL, REQUIRES MODERATE WATER MOTION, MODERATE LIGHTING AND GROWING SPACE. BELOW: *TURBINARIA* SPECIES, THE GOLDEN CUP CORAL, REQUIRES SLOW WATER MOVEMENT, MODERATE LIGHTING AND LITTLE GROWING SPACE AS IT IS NOT AGGRESSIVE.

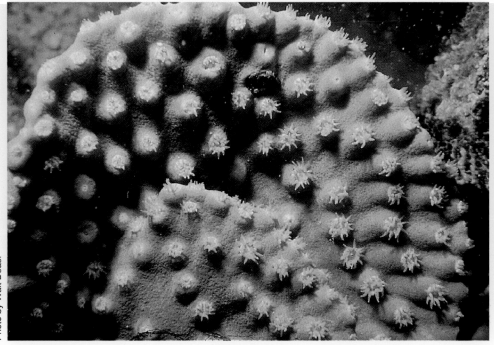

Photo by Walt Deas.

ROSE CORAL
THE GENUS *MANICINA*
Ehrenberg, 1835

The scientific name derives from the Greek *manos* meaning *wide* and *kineo* meaning *moving*. The polyps open at night and the animal lives in mud, silt, sand or attached to a hard coral. This is a popular coral in America because it is common in the Caribbean.

CARIBBEAN ROSE
CORAL, CARIBBEAN
BRAIN CORAL

MANICINA AREOLATA
Linnaeus, 1758

This is an inexpensive coral animal that is rarely sold because American hobbyists vacationing in the Caribbean or Gulf of Mexico collect their own specimens. They do very well in the aquarium with 6 hours of strong, direct light, an active water movement and lots of room. They are fast growing when happy and can kill adjoining corals when they make contact with them. These wonderful animals have an interesting characteristic. If they are in sand and a wave knocks them over, the polyp expands in the area necessary for them to return to their original position!

Collecting this coral or any coral in most Caribbean areas is forbidden. Check with the local

MANICINA AREOLATA, THE PUERTO RICAN ROSE CORAL, REQUIRES MODERATE LIGHTING, MODERATE WATER MOTION AND IS NOT TOO AGGRESSIVE.

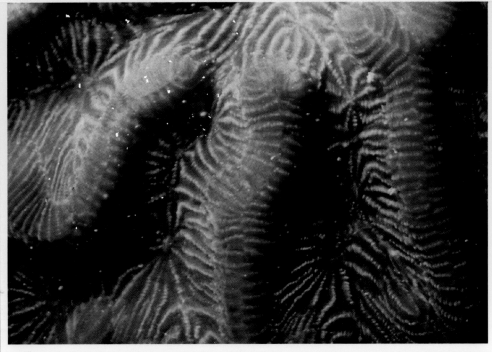

Photo by Dr. Patrick Colin.

Photo by Dr. Patrick Colin.

Manicina areolata, the Caribbean Rose as it is known in its rose-colored form.

authorities and get proper authorization before collecting any living thing on a coral reef.

THE GENUS *WELLSOPHYLLIA*
Pichon, 1980

This genus was named to honor Professor J. Wells. It appears as a hemisphere when colonized but the juveniles are convex or flat.

There is only one species and it is so variable that the designation of the entire genus is in doubt.

PACIFIC ROSE CORAL
WELLSOPHYLLIA RADIATA
Pichon 1980

This is a rare animal which has been offered in the aquarium trade. It was so rare, in fact, the only known Australian specimens were in the British Museum of Natural History

WELLSOPHYLLIA RADIATA, THE PACIFIC ROSE CORAL, CAN ONLY BE POSITIVELY IDENTIFIED BY AN EXAMINATION OF ITS UNIQUE SKELETON. OTHERWISE IT LOOKS IDENTICAL TO *MANICINA*. REQUIRES MODERATE LIGHTING, MODERATE WATER MOTION AND IS NOT TERRITORIAL.

Photo by Dr. Elizabeth M. Wood.

in London, England. Because this species ranges throughout the Philippines, Indonesia to the southerly islands of Taiwan, many of them are imported. Without checking their skeleton it is impossible to compare juveniles of this species with *Manicina* from the Caribbean. In any case their care is the same as *Manicina* and they are quite hardy.

HERPOLITHA LIMAX, THE TONGUE CORAL, REQUIRES MODERATE WATER MOVEMENT, MODERATE LIGHTING, SOME SPACE AROUND IT SO IT CAN GROW AND AN OCCASIONAL FEEDING WITH CRUSHED BABY BRINE SHRIMP. THE SMALL ROUND FLOWER ANIMAL IN THE PHOTO IS A FUNGIA.

TONGUE, SLIPPER, MOLE

THE GENUS *HERPOLITHA*
Eschscholtz, 1825

This is a very nice coral, especially when examined closely. It has very uniform structure, gets large and regenerates itself easily, often becoming Y-shaped. There are two species which range from the Red Sea to South Africa all the way around to the Marquesas. The scientific name derives from the Greek words *herpo* which means *to creep* (remember *herpetologist*) and *lithos* which means *stone*.

Photo by Dr. Elizabeth M. Wood.

Photo by Dr. Leon P. Zann.

HERPOLITHA WEBERI, THE BROWN TONGUE CORAL, REQUIRES MODERATE WATER AND LIGHT. IT IS FAIRLY AGGRESSIVE AND SHOULD BE FED ONCE A MONTH. THERE IS A GALL CRAB ON THIS SPECIMEN.

TONGUE CORAL

HERPOLITHA LIMAX
Houttuyn, 1772

This is an elongated colony that lives an isolated life on the bottom of the sea. Due to injuries it might have three or four ends and be shaped like an X or Y. The top side is convex and the bottom concave. This species has high, short septa that do not reach from the center to the outside edge. In *weberi* the corresponding septa emanate from the central groove to the perimeter, making them simple to distinguish. The polyps are only extended during the dark period of the daily cycle.

They require 6 hours of intense lighting per day, moderate water movement and room to grow as they are fast growing when they are happy. I have seen these almost 4 feet long and very heavy. They are reputed to be the heaviest of all corals due to their dense calcification.

BROWN TONGUE CORAL

HERPOLITHA WEBERI
Van der Horst, 1921

Both species of *Herpolitha* are brown and juveniles look alike (for differences see *limax*). They are very common on the Maldive

Islands where I collected hundreds of them about 5 inches long. They ship very well and are very easy to maintain in the mini-reef aquarium. They require the same care as *limax*.

SLIPPER, HAIRY SLIPPER

THE GENUS *POLYPHYLLIA*
Quoy & Gaimard, 1833

The derivation of the name is from the Greek words *polys* meaning *many* and *phyllon* meaning *leaf*. It contains one species. The polyps are elongated like seeds in a pod, not the usual round we expect. They are extended during the day. The polyps are thick and rich and cover the animal completely, thus making them attractive in the aquarium.

SLIPPER, HAIRY SLIPPER

POLYPHYLLIA TALPINA
Lamarck, 1801

There were many species in the genus *Polyphyllia* before J.E.N.Veron & Pichon (in 1980) decided they were all one species with tremendous variability. Later on (1986) John Edward Norwood Veron added two more species. Thus this coral appears in many colors and various shapes of polyps. They are widely distributed from Madagascar to Samoa. Distribution is important for aquarists. If a species is widely distributed it means it adapts

A CLOSE UP OF *HERPOLITHA LIMAX*. PHOTO BY WALT DEAS.

Photo by Dr. Elizabeth M. Wood.

ABOVE: *POLYPHYLLIA TALPINA*, THE SLIPPER CORAL, REQUIRES MODERATE LIGHTING, MODERATE WATER FLOW AND A LITTLE ROOM TO GROW. IT CAN ATTACK ADJACENT FLOWER ANIMALS.

easily and usually will make a valuable addition to the mini-reef aquarium. These are easy to care for if given enough room. They don't like too much water turbulence but they want at least 6 hours of strong light per day. All species or color varieties are cared for similarly. Look carefully at the polyps to differentiate them.

Corals have been around for many millions of years. 500 million years to be more exact. I can't think of any other complex organism that's been around that long. Maybe cockroaches? When Darwin stated that species that survive are the most fit (*Survival of the fittest!*), he didn't mean the strongest, the largest or the most beautiful. He meant the most adaptable. Animals that can adapt have learned to live under many varying circumstances. Think of coral this way: they

adapt to water temperatures from the arctic to the antarctic. They are abused by pounding waves, heated water which can suddenly be cooled, animals that kill them (Crown of Thorns, for example) and constant exposure to the sun. Many are alive only because they contain beneficial algae from which they obtain food for energy. Some are hard as a rock; some are tough as leather; some are dangerous to animals because of their strong stinging cells; some are so beautiful that they are endangered by humans who want to collect their skeletons.

THE GENUS *TUBASTREA*
Lesson, 1834

The name derives from the Latin *tubus* meaning *tube* and *astron* meaning *star*. This is a colony-growing genus with many variations in general shape. Some are shaped like trees while others are short and fluffy. Many have daylight extended polyps, but at night they are ringed with golden yellow tentacles. They require feeding of newly hatched or mashed brine shrimp. They require a lot of feeding so that each polyp receives nutrient. They are found in nature from shallows to 5,000 feet in water depth where they receive no visible light. This is important to mini-reef aquarists who must give them the shade they need. For this reason they are not recommended for beginners. They do not have zooxanthellae (algae). In nature they are frequently cave dwellers where they enjoy diminished light. These are very hungry and aggressive corals. They eat large marine worms as well as chunks of chopped food (like shrimp, fish and aquarium fish food which has ben soaked in crushed brine shrimp juice).

BELOW: *TUBASTREA COCCINEA*, THE ATLANTIC SUN CORAL, CONTAINS NO ZOOXANTHELLAE (ALGAE) SO IT DOESN'T NEED MUCH LIGHT. IT DOES REQUIRE A MODERATE WATER FLOW AND IS HIGHLY AGGRESSIVE. RIGHT: BY STUDYING THE POLYPS OF THE EXPANDED ANIMAL, YOU CAN APPRECIATE WHY THEY CALL THIS THE ATLANTIC SUN CORAL, *TUBASTREA COCCINEA*.

Photo by Walt Deas.

ATLANTIC SUN CORAL

TUBASTREA COCCINEA
Lesson, 1834

This species enjoys world-wide distribution and are quite common though they are largely ignored in most books. They can tolerate most water turbulence, though they do best in very slow moving water conditions.

They should have no direct bright light. A single fluorescent lamp is more than enough for them. They are usually orange in color.

ORANGE POLYP

TUBASTREA DIAPHANA
Dana, 1846

This Indo-pacific species looks like an orange sunburst composed of many tentacles, each widely separated emphasizing their individuality. *Each polyp must receive its own nutrition or it will die.* It only extends at night.

BELOW: *TUBASTREA DIAPHANA*, THE ORANGE POLYP CORAL HAS A VERY RARE COLOR. LOW LIGHT, MODERATE WATER MOVEMENT AND LOTS OF GROWING ROOM ARE REQUIRED.

Photos by Walt Deas.

Photos by Dr. Patrick Colin.

TUBASTREA AUREA, THE ORANGE SUN CORAL. THIS SPECIMEN WAS FROM PUERTO RICO. THE SATELLITE PHOTO SHOWS THE ANIMAL WITH ITS POLYPS RETRACTED.

ORANGE SUN CORA

TUBASTREA AUREA

A widely distributed species never reported in the aquarium literature though it is very beautiful with extremely long, orange tentacles.

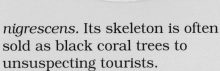

BLACK SUN CORAL

TUBASTREA MICRANTHA
Ehrenberg, 1834

This is a very dark colored, non-reef forming coral. It is the most beautiful of the genus and has fleshy tentacles and is mis-identified as *Dendrophyllia*

nigrescens. Its skeleton is often sold as black coral trees to unsuspecting tourists.

Like all *Tubastrea*, they are light shy and prefer slowly moving waters. They are not difficult to maintain but prefer their own aquarium with subdued light.

Photo by Walt Deas.

SUN, ORANGE CUP, SUNFLOWER

TUBASTREA FAULKNERI
Wells, 1982

This species does not seem to open at usual day or night schedules but is governed by its hunger. If its polyps are open all the time, it means the animal is hungry! Otherwise its care and feeding is the same as the others in the genus. I have had success feeding this coral with newly hatched fish fry and fish eggs. Each polyp must be fed individually.

TUBASTREA MICRANTHA, THE BLACK SUN CORAL, REQUIRES LOW LIGHT, MODERATE WATER MOVEMENT AND GROWING SPACE.

Expanded polyps of *Tubastrea faulkneri*.

Photo by Walt Deas.

TWO VIEWS OF *TUBASTREA FAULKNERI*. THE SUN CORAL DOESN'T NEED MUCH LIGHT, BUT DOES NEED MODERATE WATER MOTION AND GROWING SPACE.

Photo by Walt Deas.

STAGHORN,
ELKHORN CORAL

THE GENUS *ACROPORA*
Oken, 1815

The name derives from the Greek word *akron* meaning *extremity* and the Latin word *porous* meaning *pore*. This refers to the corallite at the tip of each branch. There are hundreds of species mentioned in the literature, mostly Indo-Pacific species; there are 3 or 4 Atlantic-Caribbean species each of which occupies a different ecological niche and/or range. The genus *Acropora* and the family Acroporidae are so interesting and so individualistic that a book much larger than this one would hardly contain all the available information pertaining to this interesting group. These are corals with small polyps and they are very difficult to maintain in the mini-reef aquarium. THEY ARE CERTAINLY NOT CORALS FOR BEGINNING MARINE AQUARISTS! I tried for 32 years to maintain and grow *Acropora*, mainly the Atlantic species, but with no luck. They always perished after a few months. Then I became friendly with the manufacturer of a high quality

ACROPORA FORMOSA, THE PIPE BRUSH CORAL, REQUIRES HEAVY LIGHTING, SUBSTANTIAL WATER MOVEMENT AND OCCASIONAL FEEDINGS OF LIVING BRINE SHRIMP NAUPLII. IT IS FAIRLY AGGRESSIVE AND REQUIRES EXPERT CARE.

Photo by Walt Deas.

Photo by Walt Deas.

ACROPORA FLORIDA, THE FLORIDA STAGHORN, REQUIRES HEAVY LIGHTING, HEAVY WATER MOVEMENT AND OCCASIONAL FEEDING. IT NEEDS ROOM TO GROW.

artificial sea salt. He told me that many trace elements are needed for the care of corals and, after a lot of trial and error we found that more than 33 trace elements are necessary for most corals, with strontium being most important.

They also require 8-12 hours of very strong halide lighting (though other bright lighting worked very well too) and fairly strong aeration and water movement at least for an hour per day. They thrive and reproduce in the aquarium but they never grow as well as they do in their own environment (range, habitat). If you want to

experiment, this is the group with which to work. With hundreds of nominal species, each of which easily regenerates from a piece knocked off, it is difficult to select which species to recommend. My own experiences have been with the staghorn species of the Atlantic/Caribbean, namely, *Acropora cervicornis* Lamarck,1816, *Acropora palmata* Lamarck, 1816 and *Acropora prolifera* Lamarck, 1816.

Acropora are found throughout the tropical Atlantic, Indo-Pacific and everywhere that corals grow in profusion (excluding the

Photo by Walt Deas.

ABOVE: *ACROPORA* SPECIES, ALSO KNOWN AS THE PLATE STAGHORN CORAL, REQUIRES TYPICALLY HEAVY LIGHTING AND WATER MOVEMENT. IT OCCASIONALLY WANTS TO BE FED AND REQUIRES GROWING ROOM. BELOW: *ACROPORA MILLEPORA*, THE ARMORED STAGHORN, REQUIRES HEAVY LIGHTING AND WATER MOVEMENT. IT NEEDS ROOM FOR GROWTH.

Photo by Walt Deas.

Photo by Walt Deas.

ACROPORA HUMILIS, THE PINK STAGHORN, REQUIRES SUBSTANTIAL LIGHTING (10 HOURS A DAY), HEAVY WATER MOTION AND GROWING SPACE.

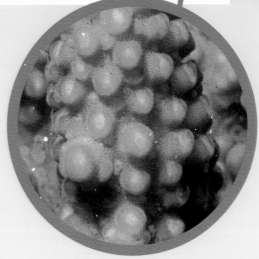

temperate and frigid zones). They are very fast growers and easily overcome their neighbors. They also are a socially structured colony where the parts of the structure grow in coordination with other parts (thus the *horns* on the staghorn and elkhorn). They are found in seven basic shapes: corymbose, digitose, caespitose, arborescent, massive, tables & plates and bottlebrush. These growths are better illustrated than described. (See accompanying illustrations pages 10-11) The identification of *Acropora* down to the species level is usually impossible with mini-reef specimens because the structure of the mature colony is part of the identification process.

They seem to do equally well whether fed or ignored as far as food is concerned. Not all have zooxanthellae.

Photo by Walt Deas.

ABOVE: *ACROPORA* SPECIES ON A REEF FLOOR. AS YET IT IS SIMPLY CALLED STAGHORN. IT REQUIRES HEAVY LIGHTING, VERY TURBULENT WATER AND GROWING SPACE. IT IS NOT RECOMMENDED FOR THE TYPICAL MINI-REEFER. BELOW: *ACROPORA* SPECIES, THE DEEP FLOOR VARIETY KNOWN AS THE AUSTRALIAN GREY, IT REPRODUCES WELL FROM SMALL PIECES. IT REQUIRES MODERATELY HEAVY LIGHTING, HEAVY WATER MOVEMENTS AND ADEQUATE GROWING ROOM.

Photo by Walt Deas.

Photo by Walt Deas.

ABOVE: *ACROPORA FORMOSA*, THE CHINESE STAGHORN, RETAINS ITS POLYPS DURING THE DAYTIME. IT IS AN IDEAL HIDING PLACE FOR FISHES AND LOBSTERS TO SAY NOTHING OF MANY INVERTEBRATES. IT DOES WELL IN THE MINI-REEF FOR AN EXPERIENCED AQUARIST WHO CAN MEET THE DEMANDS OF LOTS OF LIGHT, MASSIVE MOVEMENTS OF WATER AND GROWING ROOM. BELOW: *ACROPORA* SPECIES, THE BUSHY STAGHORN CORAL, REQUIRES MAXIMUM LIGHTING FOR 12 HOURS EACH DAY, CONSTANT WATER AGITATION AND GROWING ROOM. THESE REQUIREMENTS MAKE IT SUITABLE ONLY FOR THE ADVANCED MINI-REEFER, BUT IF YOU CAN SUPPLY THESE NEEDS, IT IS VERY REWARDING. THIS IS A NIGHT PHOTO SHOWING THE EMERGING POLYPS.

Photo by Walt Deas.

Photo by Dr. Patrick Colin.

ABOVE: *ACROPORA CERVICORNIS*, THE GREEN STAGHORN FROM THE BAHAMAS, IS A GREAT REFUGE FOR FISHES. IT REQUIRES HEAVY LIGHTING AND WATER MOTION, AND CAN BE FED EVERY WEEK OR SO. IT IS AGGRESSIVE AND REQUIRES SPACE. BELOW: *ACROPORA PROLIFERA*, THE CAT'S PAW CORAL. THIS SPECIMEN IS FROM THE BAHAMAS. IT REQUIRES 12 HOURS OF STRONG, DIRECT LIGHT, HEAVY WATER MOVEMENT AND GROWING SPACE.

Photo by Dr. Patrick Colin.

Photo by Walt Deas.

ABOVE: THIS IS THE WAY A STAGHORN CORAL GROWS ON A PROTECTED REEF SLOPE. IT TAKES OVER EVERYTHING. BELOW: THE POLYPS OF STAGHORN CORALS ARE VERY SMALL. THIS IS A NIGHT PICTURE WHEN THE POLYPS ARE EMERGED.

Photo by Walt Deas.

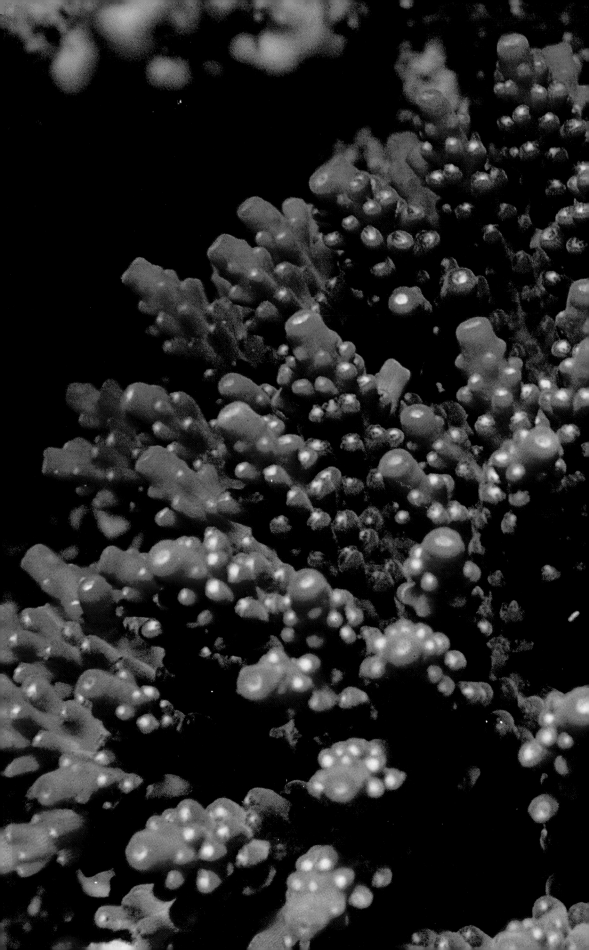

ACROPORA VALIDA, THE REDBERRY STAGHORN, IS THE MOST DESIRABLE OF ALL STAGHORNS AND ONE OF THE MOST DIFFICULT TO MAINTAIN. IT REQUIRES CONSTANT WARM TEMPERATURES OF AT LEAST 80°F, CONSTANTLY MOVING WATER AND THE EQUIVALENT OF 8 HOURS OF SUNLIGHT PER DAY. PHOTO BY WALT DEAS.

Photos by Walt Deas.

ACROPORA NOBILIS, THE PINK STAGHORN (SHOWN ABOVE) AND *ACROPORA NASUTA*, ALSO KNOWN AS THE PINK STAGHORN. BOTH SPECIES REQUIRE HEAVY LIGHTING AND WATER MOVEMENTS. THEY NEED ROOM TO GROW.

Photos by Walt Deas.

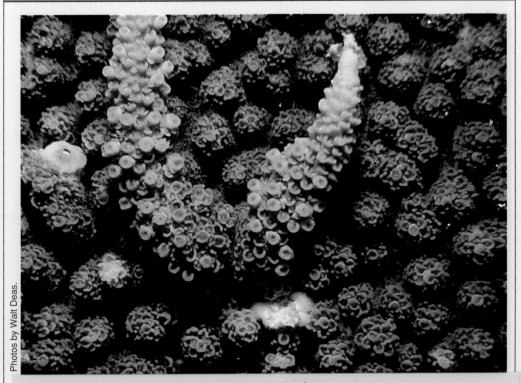

Photos by Walt Deas.

ACROPORA HYACINTHUS, THE HYACINTH CORAL (ABOVE), AND ACROPORA LORIPES, THE BLUETIP CORAL (BELOW), HAVE THE SAME REQUIREMENTS OF 8 HOURS OF SUNLIGHT OR THE EQUIVALENT, CONSTANT RAPID WATER MOVEMENT AND GROWING SPACE.

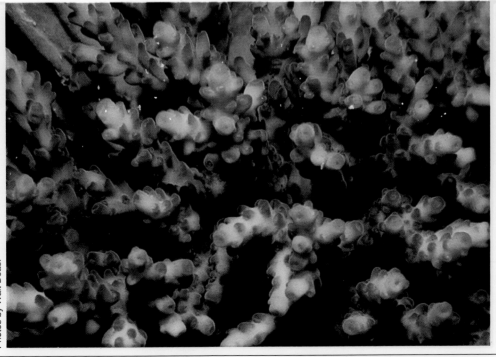

Photos by Walt Deas.

NEST, BRUSH, SERIES

THE GENUS *SERIATOPORA*
Lamarck, 1816

The name derives from the Latin *seriatus* meaning *arranged in a series*, and *porus* meaning *pore*. This is a fine, delicate coral with branches less than 1/4 inch in diameter. The branches are not neatly arranged like the staghorn or elkhorns. They are found in many colors. They are extremely hardy in their natural habitat as well as in the aquarium. They have been reported to shed healthy polyps from a colony which was dying! Another remarkable characteristic of this coral is that some of them are capable of being teased by crabs (*Hapalocarcinus marsupialis*) into creating a trap or cage from which the female cannot escape, nor can large fishes eat them. The cage has large enough spaces for the smaller male crabs to enter and fertilize the female. She raises brood after brood in the safety of her cage. Their polyps are only extended at night. There are two dozen species mentioned in the literature with less than half a dozen being true species. They are difficult to distinguish because they are so variable even in the same range and habitat.

BIRD'S NEST, CAGE CORAL

SERIATOPORA HYSTRIX
Dana, 1846

Most of my professional life has been collecting tropical fishes,

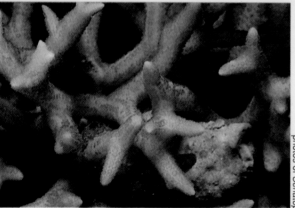

photos of *Seriatopora hystrix* by Dr. Elizabeth M. Wood.

SERIATOPORA HYSTRIX, THE BIRD'S NEST CORAL, GROWS CLOSE TO THE SURFACE IN NATURE SO IT NEEDS 8 HOURS OF SUNLIGHT PER DAY, PLUS TURBULENT WATER AND LOTS OF ROOM TO GROW. IT IS EXTREMELY DIFFICULT TO KEEP ALIVE IF THESE CONDITIONS ARE NOT SUPPLIED. IF, HOWEVER, YOU CAN SUPPLY THE NECESSARY CONDITIONS, IT WILL THRIVE.

Photo by Walt Deas.

SERIATOPORA HYSTRIX WITH CRAB GALLS. THE CRAB FORCES THE CORAL TO FORM A CAGE AROUND THE FEMALE CRAB WHO SPENDS THE REST OF HER LIFE AS A PRISONER OF THE CORAL. THE MALES ARE MUCH SMALLER THAN THE FEMALE AND THEY CAN ENTER OR LEAVE THE GALL WITHOUT DIFFICULTY.

photographing them and bringing them back alive. Catching reef fishes isn't always easy but with help of *hystrix* it made the job a lot easier in the Fiji Islands. Not only do the branches of the colony harbor crabs, but they are a refuge for small fishes which hide among the many possible crevices afforded by *hystrix*. This coral occurs throughout the range of the genus and may be blue, green, pink or cream. It is a very common species close to the surface of the water, thus its need for 8 hours of strong light per day in a turbulent water situation. Its branches taper and may be very

pointed, bifurcated (two points to the branch end) and shows mishandling easily. The broken ends may be used for reproduction but they seriously affect the health of the animal. Under the correct conditions, this is a valuable addition to the mini-reef aquarium. The growth tips of the branches are usually white.

BRUSH CORAL
SERIATOPORA CALIENDRUM
Ehrenberg, 1834

This coral is a thicker edition of *hystrix*. It grows in the same helter-skelter manner but its

Photo by Walt Deas.

SERIATOPORA CALIENDRUM, THE BRUSH CORAL, REQUIRES HEAVY LIGHTING, HEAVY WATER MOVEMENT AND MINIMAL SEPARATION FROM OTHER FLOWER ANIMALS. IF YOU CAN SUPPLY THE PHYSICAL NEEDS, THE ANIMAL WILL PROSPER; IF YOU CAN'T, THE ANIMAL WILL PROBABLY PERISH.

branches are four times thicker and they do not taper. They are much less delicate than *hystrix* but require the same care. They are easier to care for because they have physically stronger branches and ship easier.

coral varies in shape from blunt-tipped branches to an amorphous (without shape) mass. There are twenty four nominal species (in name only) but because of the great variation in shape, there might only be four true species with lots of variations.

CAT'S PAW, STUMP CORAL, CLUB FOOT CORAL, GYPSY CORAL

THE GENUS *STYLOPHORA*
Schweigger, 1819

The derivation of the name is from the Greek words *stylos* which has several meanings but in this case means *pillar* and *phero* which means *to carry*. This

GYPSY CORAL, CLUB FOOT

STYLOPHORA PISTILLATA
Esper, 1797

Their branches have round, thick ends which may be 1/2 inch in diameter. Their color seems to be uniformly cream or tan, bright purple or pink. The tips of the branches may be white if the coral is actively growing. This is a

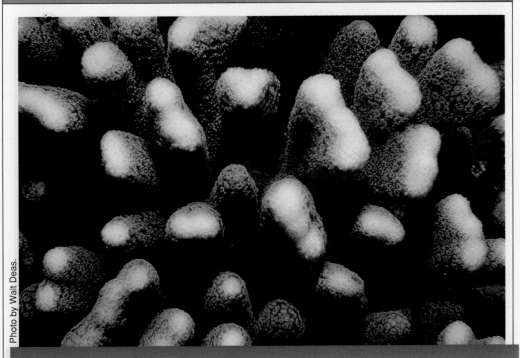

Photo by Walt Deas.

STYLOPHORA PISTILLATA, THE CLUBFOOT CORAL OR THE GYPSY CORAL, IS VERY DIFFICULT TO CARE FOR AND ONLY VERY EXPERIENCED MINI-REEFERS SHOULD ATTEMPT TO KEEP THEM ALIVE. THEY REQUIRE 12 HOURS OF SUNLIGHT, HEAVY WATER MOVEMENTS AND A LITTLE GROWING ROOM.

bothersome animal to keep in the mini-reef aquarium and is usually not worth the effort from the point of view of beauty. It requires 8 hours of strong light per day with moving water continuously cleansing its branches. Tiny polyps emerge at night and feeding is not necessary.

They are everywhere numerous and breed easily in nature. Pregnant females release internally fertilized planulae (free-swimming larvae) which attach to anything hard, like pieces of floating wood (like barnacles). This enables them to be transported all over the world and become quite common. They reproduce from pieces broken off the colony.

STYLOPHORA PISTILLATA AND CRAB GALLS. THE NORMALLY ROUNDED END OF THE CORAL HAS BEEN MODIFIED INTO A HOLLOW CAGE FOR THE FEMALE GALL CRAB. SHE REMAINS IMPRISONED HER ENTIRE LIFE. THE SLIT IS LARGE ENOUGH FOR THE MALE GALL CRABS TO ENTER AND LEAVE.

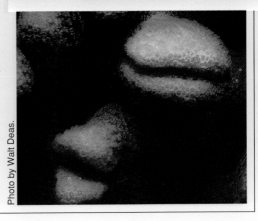

Photo by Walt Deas.

STYLOPHORA PISTILLATA.
PHOTO BY WALT DEAS.

CACTUS CORAL, PEACOCK

THE GENUS *PAVONA*
Lamarck, 1801

This coral forms various colonies which have shapes from heads of lettuce (foliaceous) to clumps to cat's paw. They are variously colored in gray, cream, pink, purple, green or yellow with lighter growing tips. They have tiny tentacles, smaller than 1/25 of an inch which are extended during the day. These are difficult corals to identify from other members of the family Agaraciidae.

The literature includes some 50 nominal species, but only 12 are recognized as true species. They range throughout the tropical and more temperate waters except in the Atlantic. There are huge colonies in southern Japan and southern California.

LETTUCE CLUMP CORAL

PAVONA VENOSA
Ehrenberg, 1834

This tan species seems to bridge the leafy and the clumping forms of the genus. It sometimes has tinges of yellow, light green and pink, but is never very attractive. It is fairly difficult to keep alive as it require 8 hours of strong light per day, moderately heavy water movement and lots of room.

PAVONA VENOSA, THE LETTUCE CLUMP CORAL, REQUIRES HEAVY LIGHTING, HEAVY WATER MOTION AND LOTS OF GROWING SPACE.

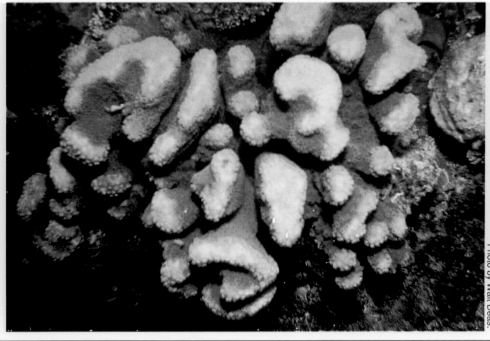

Photo by Walt Deas.

Pavona decussata.

PAVONA DECUSSATA, THE CACTUS CORAL, REQUIRES 10 HOURS OF SUNLIGHT OR ITS EQUIVALENT, HEAVY WATER MOVEMENT AND SOME GROWING ROOM.

distributed worldwide and does well in the aquarium under 8 hours of strong light and not touching any other coral.

CACTUS COLUMN CORAL

PAVONA CLAVUS
Dana, 1846

This species forms colonies either in the shape of a table or of a cactus or column. They are not remarkably colored in a creamy color which might even be tan. It is well

PAVONA CLAVUS, THE CACTUS COLUMN CORAL. THIS SPECIMEN IS FROM SABAH, MALAYSIA. IT REQUIRES 8 HOURS OF SUNLIGHT OR ITS EQUIVALENT (IF THERE IS SUCH A THING!), HEAVY WATER MOVEMENT AND SOME GROWING ROOM.

CACTUS, BRAIN CORAL, DAISY CORAL

PAVONA DECUSSATA
Dana, 1846

These corals are irregularly shaped leaves which stand upright. They are best described by a photo. Their natural color is green, brown or golden yellow. They do well in the mini-reef aquarium because they are easy to ship. Huge quantities come out of Singapore. They are difficult to maintain without 10 hours of very strong light per day, heavy water motion and a clean tank. Debris seems to clog their beautiful, tiny daisy-shaped polyps.

Pavona decussata.

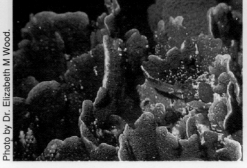

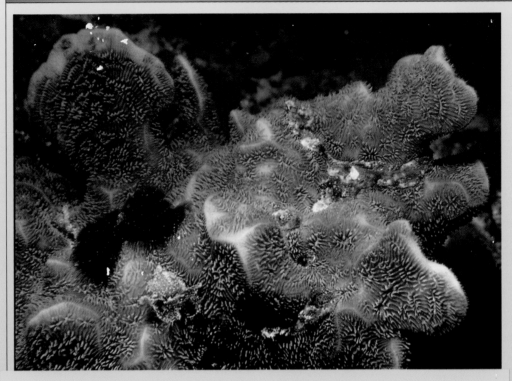

ABOVE: *PAVONA DECUSSATA*. BELOW: WALT DEAS WITH *PAVONA MINUTA*. THIS SPECIES HAS NOT BEEN KEPT IN A MINI-REEF AQUARIUM BUT DOES WELL IN VERY LARGE TANKS UNDER THE SAME PARAMETERS AS OTHER *PAVONA* SPECIES.

Photo by Jean Deas.

Photo by Walt Deas.

PAVONA *CACTUS*, THE FRILLY CACTUS, REQUIRES 8 HOURS OF SUNLIGHT (OR ITS EQUIVALENT), HEAVY WATER MOTION, AND JUST A BIT OF ROOM FOR EXPANSION AS IT IS NOT AGGRESSIVE. IT GROWS IN HEAVY PATCHES WHEN YOU ARE SUCCESSFUL.

FRILLY CACTUS,
LETTUCE, TWISTED LEATHER CORAL

PAVONA CACTUS
ForskÅl, 1775

In their natural biotope, these cactus-like corals develop into huge colonies which can be 40 feet in diameter if they have no opposition.

They are not colorful being mostly tan, brown or green/brown. They require 8 hours of intense lighting, constant water movement and no feeding. They don't seem to mind being crowded, even though they develop huge colonies in nature. A close look at the colonies indicate it wants to be branched but the branches turn to leaves.

***PAVONA VARIANS*, THE BRAIN CACTUS CORAL, DEMANDS 10 HOURS SUNLIGHT (OR EQUIVALENT) AND VERY ACTIVE WATER MOTIONS TO SURVIVE. IT IS A TEST CORAL FOR BEGINNERS WHO THINK THEY HAVE THE KNOW-HOW TO ADVANCE WITH A MORE DIFFICULT SPECIES. BELOW IS THE DRIED POTATO CACTUS, *PAVONA* SPECIES, WITH THE SAME REQUIREMENTS AS *PAVONA VARIANS*.**

Photos by Walt Deas.

HORN CORAL, BRANCH, KNOB CORAL

THE GENUS *HYDNOPHORA*
Fischer de Waldheim, 1807

The name derives from the Greek words *hydnon* which means *tuber* and *phero* which means *to carry*. There are 22 species mentioned in the literature, but in reality there are but 5 species with real variability. They are easily and remarkably identified by the serrated, cone-shaped parts which develop between the centers of the corallites (hydnophores). They are well distributed over the entire Indo-Pacific including the Red Sea. If you have a low power (12X) microscope, have a close look at the hydnophores. All species require 8 hours of strong light per day; even more won't hurt. They are highly aggressive and extremely difficult to keep in the mini-reef aquarium as are all corals with small polyps. Their tiny tentacles are extended during the day if the corals are happy.

HORN CORAL

HYDNOPHORA RIGIDA
Dana, 1846

Colonies are like trees (arborescent) with branches growing

Close up of *Hydnophora rigida*. Photo by Walt Deas.

EVEN MORE DIFFICULT TO MAINTAIN SUCCESSFULLY ARE THE HORN CORALS OF THE GENUS *HYDNOPHORA*. THE MOST POPULAR SPECIES IS *HYDNOPHORA RIGIDA*, THE HORN CORAL, WHICH LOOKS LIKE A TANGLED MASS SIMILAR TO THE *ACROPORA*. THEY REQUIRE 8 HOURS OF VERY BRIGHT LIGHTING, HEAVY WATER AGITATION AND THEY ARE TERRIBLY AGGRESSIVE. THEY USUALLY DESTROY ANY FLOWER ANIMAL WITH WHICH THEY MAKE CONTACT.

Photo by Dr. Elizabeth M. Wood.

in all directions, giving small fishes, crabs and snails a safe place in which to hide. They are found in cream, tan, brown and sometimes green. Their branches have no common base. I found massive colonies in the Fiji Islands in shallow lagoons. The hydnophores are large lumps on the branches.

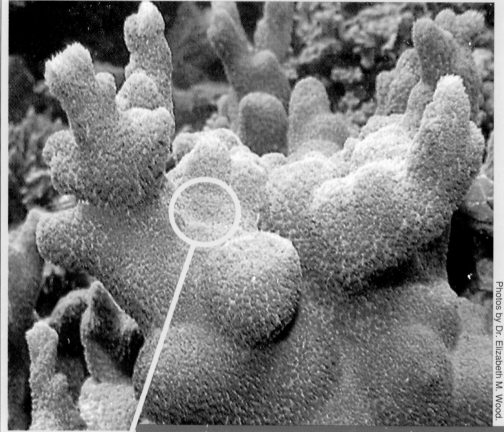

Photos by Dr. Elizabeth M. Wood.

HYDNOPHORA PILOSA, THE KNOB HORN CORAL, IS ONLY FOR ADVANCED MINI-REEFERS. IT REQUIRES HEAVY LIGHTING AND WATER MOVEMENT. IT CANNOT BE CLOSE TO OTHER CORALS AS IT KILLS THEM.

KNOB CORAL
HYDNOPHORA PILOSA
Veron, 1985

This relatively new species was created by the outstanding reef scientist John Edward Norwood Veron from specimens originating on Elizabeth Reef, eastern Australia. These encrusting species have thick bases and travel easily which makes them candidates for the mini-reef aquarium. Australian hobbyists say they are not too difficult to maintain with 10 hours of bright light per day. They do not want water agitation, but appreciate slow-moving water constantly bathing their perpetually extended polyps (day and night).

Photos by Walt Deas.

HYDNOPHORA EXESA, THE HORNY BRANCH CORAL, REQUIRES 10 HOURS OF SUNLIGHT OR ITS EQUIVALENT, RAPID WATER MOVEMENT AND ISOLATION FOR GROWTH.

HORNY BRANCH CORAL, HORN CORAL

HYDNOPHORA EXESA
Pallas, 1766

This is an aquarium favorite because it has a wide range around Indonesia and the Philippines (places from which it is shipped world-wide). It is a dirty green or brown and is not particularly interesting except for the pleasure of cultivating an extremely difficult species. It is a shallow water species, found in lagoons which makes it easy to collect. It requires 10 hours of strong light per day, moderately heavy water movement and no feeding.

Photos by Dr. Elizabeth M. Wood and Walt Deas

HYDNOPHORA MICROCONUS, THE YELLOW HORN CORAL, IS THE MOST COMPATIBLE SPECIES IN THE GENUS FOR THE MINI-REEFER. IT NEEDS LOTS OF INTENSE LIGHT AND WATER MOVEMENT, BUT IT THRIVES IF THESE PHYSICAL REQUIREMENTS ARE SUPPLIED. YOU STILL HAVE TO HAVE A LOT OF EXPERIENCE WITH CORALS TO SUCCEED WITH ANY OF THE HORN CORALS.

YELLOW HORN
HYDNOPHORA MICROCONUS
Lamarck, 1816

This is the coral for the large mini-reef. It forms huge clumps which travel well since the polyps are so small. It is dull green or tan and is everywhere rare.
Specimens are sometimes shipped from Israel as small pieces which, if properly cared for, grow well.

They need lots of light, strong water movement and no physical contact with more aggressive corals.

PORITES SPECIES, THE JEWEL CORALS, ARE VERY DIFFICULT TO MAINTAIN AND ARE NOT RECOMMENDED FOR THE BEGINNER. WHEN BEGINNERS ARE READY TO TRY THEIR SKILLS ON MORE DIFFICULT FLOWER ANIMALS, THIS IS THE GENUS TO TACKLE. THEY NEED 10-12 HOURS OF BRIGHT LIGHT EVERY DAY WITH VERY HEAVY WATER MOVEMENT. THEY CAN STAND CROWDING AND ARE NOT A DANGER TO THEIR CORAL NEIGHBORS. THEY HAVE BEEN CALLED *JEWEL* CORALS BECAUSE THEIR CORALLITES LOOK LIKE JEWELS TO SOME PEOPLE (NOT TO ME!).

FINGER CORAL, PORITES, JEWELED CORALS, HONEYCOMB CORAL

THE GENUS *PORITES*
Link, 1807

The name derives from the Latin word *porus* meaning *pore* and the Greek *ites* which, when added to the end of a word denotes similarity. They colonize into many shapes and many colors, but basically they are brown. Green, red, blue, purple and yellow are often seen. Polyps are rarely opened during the daytime. Their tentacles are tiny and are barely visible. Calices are uniformly shaped (thus the honeycomb designation), sometimes even circular, with common walls. The genus is distributed completely around the temperate and tropical zones where corals are to be found. They achieve this massive distribution by reproducing sexually. The female's eggs are fertilized internally by sperm released by other *Porites* of the same species. The eggs incubate and, when sufficiently developed, are released as free swimming larvae (planulae). They attach to the first solid thing they strike, be it another hard coral or a piece of floating styrofoam. The lucky ones are carried on a piece of wood in the warm current to their new habitat where they eventually fall off their transport and establish themselves properly.

The study of these corals from a systematic point of view is impossible. You can only study them geographically, thus you can differentiate between all of the *Porites* of the Maldive Islands and give them valid names only to find the identical coral a thousand miles away. There are 125 species recorded and no one knows how many are valid because current techniques for identifying corals are insufficient. Molecular biology will probably solve the *Porites* problem for us. Up to now scientists have relied upon the shape of the colony but they all know that such a reliance is probably faulty.

Many years ago (1952) I brought back two species (?) from the Caribbean island of Nassau. The coral lived for a few months in my aquarium but slowly died as the lack of trace elements took its toll. But the big surprise for me was the explosion of beautifully colored fan worms (serpulids). At that time I was in

PORITES SPECIES, THE BLUE JEWEL CORAL, DOES NOT REQUIRE AS MUCH LIGHT AS THE OTHER PORITES, BUT IT DOES NEED 6-8 HOURS OF BRIGHT LIGHT PER DAY WITH LOTS OF WATER MOVEMENT.

Photo by MP&C Piednoir Aqua Press.

Photo by Walt Deas.

PORITES SPECIES, THE GOLDEN JEWEL CORAL, IS FOUND IN VERY SHALLOW WATER IN A PROTECTED REEF AREA. THIS SPECIES NEEDS LOTS OF LIGHT (10 HOURS OF SUNLIGHT PER DAY), BUT NOT TOO MUCH WATER AGITATION.

the tropical fish business so I imported large quantities of these *Porites*, almost all of which were infected with these colorful worms. Imports of *Porites* from other parts of the world also produced these worms which had bored into their skeleton. I called these *Porites* **living rocks** because not only were the corals living but so were the worms. The modern name for these infested *Porites* is Christmas Tree Worm Rock. When they grow in staghorn-shaped colonies, they become refuges for small reef animals like fishes, crabs, etc.

These are VERY DIFFICULT corals to maintain. They require intense light 8-10 hours a day, extremely agitated water

movements and lots of room. Those requirements are not conducive to a beautiful mini-reef aquarium! However, if you can dedicate the space and provide the light and water movement, the tree-like species are strongly growing and quickly fill the mini-reef aquarium.

The colors of *Porites* are universal. They are found in purple, orange, pink, red, yellow, green, brown, cream and even white. Unlike most stony corals, *Porites* shed periodically. This is probably the food eaten by the fan worms. It also has something to do with water movement because the faster the water moves around them the less they shed.

Since all *Porites* require

Photo by Walt Deas.

PORITES, THE RUSTY JEWEL CORAL, PERIODICALLY SHEDS ITS WAXY COAT TO THE DETRIMENT OF OTHER CORAL ANIMALS. HEAVY WATER MOVEMENT AND LIGHTING ARE REQUIRED TO MAINTAIN THIS SPECIES. THIS MINI-ATOLL WAS LOCATED IN A PROTECTED LAGOON.

PORITES CYLINDRICA, THE FINGER JEWEL CORAL, WITH DIVER JEAN DEAS TO SHOW THE MASSIVENESS OF THIS CORAL HEAD. IT REQUIRES LOTS OF LIGHT AND WATER MOVEMENT AS DO MOST OF THE MEMBERS OF THIS GENUS.

basically the same care and their identification is so tenuous, identifications through photographs is the acceptable method used in the mini-reef aquarium hobby.

Photo by Walt Deas.

Photo by Cathy Church.

PORITES LUTEA WITH CHRISTMAS TREE WORMS, *SPIROBRANCHUS GIGANTEUS*, HAS EARNED THIS *PORITES* THE NAME CHRISTMAS TREE WORM ROCK. UNFORTUNATELY THERE ARE MANY SUCH CORALS IN THE GENUS AS THESE WORMS SELECT ANY *PORITES* AVAILABLE. AS THE *PORITES* IS SO DIFFICULT TO MAINTAIN, SO ARE THE WORMS WHICH INFECT THEM. WHEN THE CORAL DIES SO DO THE WORMS! THESE WORMS ARE ALSO REFERRED TO AS FEATHER DUSTER WORMS; THEY ARE VERY SENSITIVE AND IRREGULAR WATER MOVEMENTS, STRONG LIGHT OR SOUNDS MAKES THEM WITHDRAW.

Photo by Walt Deas.

ABOVE: *PORITES ANNAE*, THE HAND JEWEL CORAL, DOES FAIRLY WELL WITH SOME EXPERTS AND POORLY WITH OTHERS. SOME BEGINNERS EVEN HAVE SUCCESS...*BEGINNER'S LUCK*, THEY SAY. IN ANY CASE THEY DON'T DO WELL WITHOUT 8-10 HOURS OF DIRECT SUNLIGHT (OR ITS EQUIVALENT), MASSIVE MOVEMENTS OF WATER AND THE COMPANY OF SMALL FISHES.
BELOW: *PORITES ANTENNUATA*, THE JEWELED TOE CORAL, HAS THE SAME HARSH REQUIREMENTS AS MOST *PORITES*. HEAVY WATER MOVEMENTS, 10-12 HOURS OF SUNLIGHT OR ITS EQUIVALENT IN ARTIFICIAL LIGHTING, AND NO DEMANDS ON LIVING SPACE ARE REQUIREMENTS TO MAINTAIN THIS FLOWER ANIMAL.

Photo by Walt Deas.

Photo by Walt Deas.

Above: **Porites** and **Millepora** can thrive together. Below: **Porites cylindrica**, the Finger Jewel Coral.

Photo by Walt Deas.

PORITES LOBATA, THE TURTLE JEWEL CORAL, IS EXTREMELY DIFFICULT TO MAINTAIN IN THE MINI-REEF AQUARIUM. IT REQUIRES 12 HOURS OF SUNLIGHT OR ITS ARTIFICIAL EQUIVALENT AND HEAVY WATER MOTION. IT IS NOT AGGRESSIVE BUT I HAVE ONLY SEEN IT SUCCESSFULLY CULTIVATED IN LARGE PUBLIC AQUARIUMS WHICH HAVE RUNNING SEA WATER.

Photo by Walt Deas.

PORITES LUTEA, THE CHRISTMAS TREE WORM ROCK, IS THE PREFERRED *PORITES* FOR THE CHRISTMAS TREE WORM, *SPIROBRANCHUS GIGANTEUS.*

Photo by Walt Deas.

BOWL, BIRD'S NEST, CAULIFLOWER, LACE, BRUSH, CLUSTER CORAL, WART CORAL

THE GENUS *POCILLOPORA*
Lamarck, 1816

The name derives from the Latin words *pocillum* which means *bowl* and *porus* meaning *pore*.

Most of the species in this genus are fingered or tree-like and the names used by hobbyists describe these forms. This is one of the most problematic of the small polyped corals for maintenance in the mini-reef. Different species have differing requirements but it seems that they are best suited to the same physical conditions under which they were cultivated or existed naturally. There is considerable aquaculture of these corals at the present time.

Colors vary from brown, green and yellow, but most of the aquarium specimens are pink or orange. Their branches have well-rounded tips and are bushy which gives them the name Cauliflower Coral, but there are many fingered species which form the miraculous cages in which the gall crab (*Hapalocarcinus marsupialis*) is imprisoned (protected?).

The literature contains references to 35 species.

CAULIFLOWER, WART CORAL

POCILLOPORA DAMICORNIS
Linnaeus, 1758

Photo by Dr. Elizabeth M. Wood.

AN AMAZING PHOTO, IT SHOWS A GALL CRAB *HAPALOCARCINUS MARSUPIALIS* ENTRAPPED FOR ITS LIFETIME IN THE TIP OF THE BRANCH OF *POCILLOPORA DAMICORNIS* CORAL. THE MALE GALL CRABS ARE SMALL ENOUGH TO CRAWL IN AND OUT OF THE SLIT IN THE CORAL TIP TO MATE WITH THE FEMALE.

This species, or one similar to it, is being produced now at five aquaculture facilities around the world (or so they say!). This makes it less expensive and more reliable than wild caught Cauliflowers. The polyps are rather large and resemble the rosettes of a cauliflower. These are not simple corals to maintain. None of the short polyped corals are, for that matter. They require 8 hours of intense lighting, agitated water movements and should not be

Photo by Dr. Gerald R. Allen and Roger Steene.

POCILLOPORA DAMICORNIS, THE CAULIFLOWER CORAL. IT REQUIRES 8 HOURS OF BRIGHT LIGHT AND VERY HEAVY WATER MOVEMENT. IT SHOULD NOT BE ADJACENT TO ANY OTHER FLOWER ANIMALS.

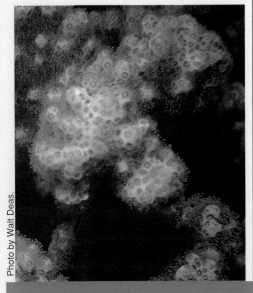

Photo by Walt Deas.

touching other corals. The verrucae (worts) meld into the branches. This melding depends upon the water agitation. The more water agitation the more closely placed and compact are the branches. These are very common in every biotope. Appears in pink, tan, cream, brown and green.

POCILLOPORA SPECIES, THE BLUSHING CAULIFLOWER CORAL, IS VERY DIFFICULT TO MAINTAIN IN CAPTIVITY...BUT SO WERE ALL CORALS IN 1980! THIS ONE REQUIRES LOTS OF LIGHT, UP TO 12 HOURS A DAY, AND HEAVY WATER MOVEMENT. IT SHOULD NOT BE ADJACENT TO OTHER FLOWER ANIMALS.

Pocillopora damicornis, the Cauliflower Coral, with two crab galls.

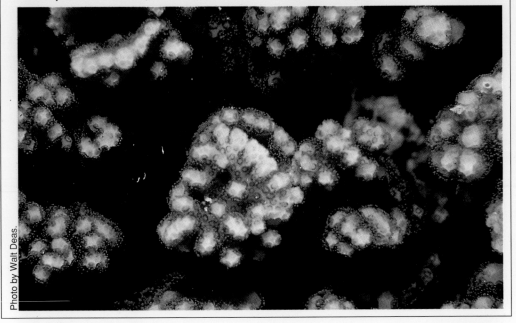

Photo by Walt Deas.

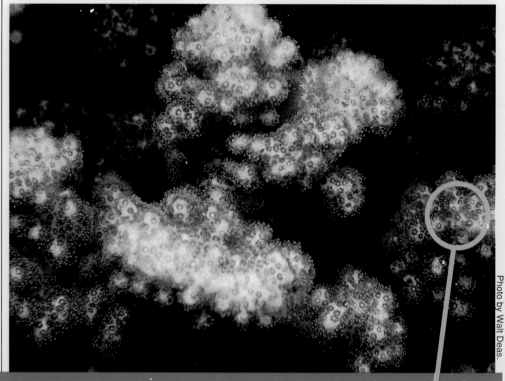

Photo by Walt Deas.

POCILLOPORA VERRUCOSA, THE PINK CAULIFLOWER, REQUIRES 10 HOURS OF INTENSE LIGHT AND HEAVY WATER MOVEMENT. IT SHOULD NOT BE ADJACENT TO OTHER FLOWER ANIMALS.

PINK WART, PINK CAULIFLOWER CORAL

POCILLOPORA VERRUCOSA
Ellis & Solander, 1786

This very common coral requires a tremendous amount of light and is, therefore, only found in shallow reef environments. It also is subjected to heavy seas, so these are the conditions which must be met for successful aquarium culture. Its colors usually vary from skin-pink to heavy cream, but blue, green and brown specimens are found more rarely. It is very similar to *damicornis*. It ranges from the Red

Pocillopora verrucosa from Sabah, Malaysia.

Sea south to East Africa thence to Hawaii and around Australia. The branches do not meld into the warts as they do in *damicornis*. With 10 hours of intense light and greatly agitated water you have a fair chance of success in culturing this species.

Photo by Dr. Elizabeth M. Wood.

Pocillopora verrucosa, the Pink Cauliflower Coral is not always pink!

POCILLOPORA SPECIES, THE PINK WART CAULIFLOWER CORAL REQUIRES 10 HOURS OF INTENSE LIGHT AND HEAVY WATER MOVEMENTS. IT IS VERY DIFFICULT TO MAINTAIN FOR LONG PERIODS OF TIME PROBABLY BECAUSE OF ITS NEED FOR CERTAIN TRACE ELEMENTS, BUT THIS IS JUST SPECULATION ON MY PART.

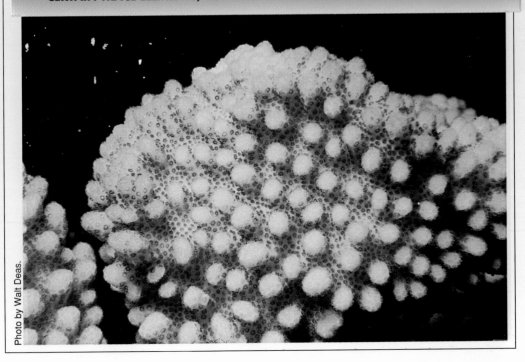

Photo by Walt Deas.

Photo by Dr. Elizabeth M. Wood.

PECTINIA SPECIES, THE GOLD CARNATION CORAL, NEEDS 8 HOURS OF INTENSE LIGHT AND FAIRLY HEAVY WATER MOVEMENTS, BUT IT IS STILL THE MOST DIFFICULT OF CORALS TO MAINTAIN IN THE MINI-REEF AQUARIUM.

HIBISCUS CORAL,
LETTUCE, CARNATION CORAL

THE GENUS *PECTINIA*
Oken, 1815

The name derives from the Greek word *pectinis* meaning *comb* which describes the elongated, delicate walls. The forms of this coral may be lettuce-like, encrusting or branched. The polyps are brown or grey, sometimes pink or green, and the tentacles, which are shown only at night, may be lighter. The colonies reach 4 feet in diameter and occur in various depths of water. Several coral scientists think they are the most beautifully colored corals with their red, blues, greens and pinks. There are seven species but 14 nominal (in name only in the literature) species. The polyps are nocturnal but even at night they open for only a very short time.

ANTLER LETTUCE,
HIBISCUS CORAL

PECTINIA ALCICORNIS
Saville-Kent, 1871

This coral grows in a solid mass and is probably mis-identified by many dealers who think of it as an antler or branching variety, which it may look like when it is marginally alive. It occurs in khaki colors with more yellow occasionally. This is widely distributed from Indonesia (where most supplies are collected) to Australia. They require lots of light, heavy water agitation and are extremely difficult to keep from imported

Photo by Dr. Elizabeth M. Wood.

PECTINIA ALCICORNIS, THE ANTLER LETTUCE, REQUIRES 10 HOURS OF INTENSE LIGHT PER DAY AND HEAVY WATER MOVEMENT. LIKE ALL *PECTINIA*, THIS IS A DIFFICULT FLOWER ANIMAL TO MAINTAIN.

specimens. If you can find a local mini-reefer doing well with them, get some. They do well when they travel short distances. Truly, you should only buy corals from dealer's mini-reefs where the corals are healthy and acclimated.

Photo by Dr. Elizabeth M. Wood.

PECTINIA PAEONIA, THE HIBISCUS LETTUCE CORAL, IS VERY DIFFICULT TO MAINTAIN AS ARE ALL PECTINIA. HEAVY WATER MOVEMENT AND 10 HOURS OF INTENSE LIGHTING ARE MINIMAL REQUIREMENTS, BUT THEY ARE NOT AN AGGRESSIVE SPECIES.

HIBISCUS CORAL, PALM LETTUCE CORAL

PECTINIA PAEONIA
Dana, 1846

This is not an attractive coral and is difficult to keep alive, so why bother? Because it is often sold from Sri Lanka along with other corals. It has a light, dirty tan complexion with a strong build. Strong teeth decorate the costa. These are very common corals in turbid areas where the bottom is constantly stirred up. It needs a lot of light; 8 hours a day is minimum.

CARNATION CORAL, FRILLY LETTUCE

PECTINIA LACTUCA
Pallas, 1766

It is difficult to maintain this coral in your mini-reef aquarium unless you know the conditions in

Photo by Dr. Elizabeth M. Wood.

PECTINIA SPECIES FROM SABAH, MALAYSIA, OFTEN CALLED THE WITHERED LETTUCE, REQUIRES THE SAME CARE AS PECTINIA ALCICORNIS.

which it existed prior to your acquisition. They do well in saturated light of 10 hours duration per day. Some like turbid conditions while others like placid habitats. They have small polyps and tiny tentacles which extend some nights (not all nights). My success has always been using heavily active waters and bright light (10 hours). They have very interesting shapes but uninteresting colors.

PECTINIA LACTUCA, THE FRILLY LETTUCE OR CARNATION CORAL, IS DIFFICULT TO MAINTAIN. IT MUST HAVE 10 HOURS OF INTENSE LIGHT PER DAY AND HEAVY WATER MOVEMENT CONSTANTLY.

Photo by MP&C Piednoir Aqua Press.

THE SKELETON OF *PECTINIA LACTUCA*,
THE FRILLY LETTUCE CORAL, IS JUST AS
BEAUTIFUL AS THE LIVING ANIMAL.
SKELETONS ARE NECESSARY TO VERIFY
IDENTIFICATIONS. PHOTO BY DR.
HERBERT R. AXELROD.

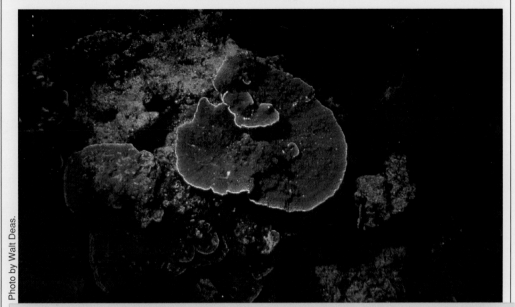

Photo by Walt Deas.

MONTIPORA CAPRICORNIS, THE SALAD BOWL CORAL, OCCURS IN VERY DEEP WATERS AS WELL AS IN DEPTHS OF 15-20 FEET. BUT THEIR MINI-REEF AQUARIUM NEEDS ARE THE SAME: 8-10 HOURS.

VELVET CORALS, WHITE MOUNTAIN CORAL

THE GENUS *MONTIPORA*
De Blainville, 1830

The name derives from the Latin words *mons* meaning *mountain* and *porus* meaning *pore*.

A close study of the tubercles which are mountain-like (in miniature of course) and the tentacles, which are white, inspired the Latin name. This is a huge genus of corals which exist over a great part of the coral-bearing world excluding the Americas. They exist in most coral shapes and most coral colors. Obviously, then, they are difficult to identify (by the scientists as well as the mini-reefer). Because of their lack of spectacle, they are not often studied by the few coral specialists around the world. They are impossible to identify by photographs. Even the skeleton must be studied by an expert, thus the names given are mostly educated guesses. All 211

MONTIPORA CAPRICORNIS, THE SALAD BOWL CORAL, IN ITS FOLIACEOUS FORM. THIS CORAL APPEARS IN OTHER FORMS AS WELL BUT THEY ALL REQUIRE 8-10 HOURS OF INTENSE LIGHT PER DAY, MODERATE WATER MOVEMENT AND CAN SAFELY BE ADJACENT TO OTHER FLOWER ANIMALS.

Photo by Dr. Elizabeth M. Wood.

Photo by Walt Deas.

Montipora capricornis, the Salad Bowl Coral.

Montipora stellata.

Photo by Walt Deas.

MONTIPORA STELLATA.
PHOTO BY WALT DEAS.

nominal species require 8 hours of intense light per day with semi-turbid water and slightly higher water temperatures of 80°F. and above. Even under these conditions they are far from easy to culture.

SALAD BOWL CORAL

MONTIPORA CAPRICORNIS
Veron, 1985

This species is only found in Australia and it is a phenomenal species if you can keep it in a large aquarium. It comes in solid colors such as blue, purple, tan or cream. It often occurs in two forms in the same colony like finger and table at the same time. It needs 8 hours of intense light and slowly moving waters.

VELVET CORAL, FINGER CORAL

MONTIPORA VERRUCOSA
Lamarck, 1816

This looks like a very fuzzy, cuddly coral. They are completely covered with tubercles which give it the velvety appearance. Their aquamarine polyps are extended during the daylight hours. They need 8 hours of daylight at a minimum and moderate water turbulence. They are found in most coral colors.

VELVET FINGER CORAL

MONTIPORA DIGITATA
Dana, 1846

This widespread species is very distinctive and has lovely little

Montipora verrucosa.

Photo by Walt Deas.

Photos by Dr. Elizabeth M. Wood and Walt Deas.

MONTIPORA DIGITATA, THE VELVET FINGER CORAL, IS A DELICATE CORAL AND THE FINGERS BREAK EASILY MAKING IT DIFFICULT TO TRANSPORT. IT REQUIRES 7 HOURS OF STRONG LIGHT PER DAY WITH SUBSTANTIAL WATER MOVEMENT.

THESE LEAFY AND PLATE-LIKE CORALS FOUND IN 20 FEET OF WATER IN SABAH, MALAYSIA ARE CALLED MONTIPORA SPONGODES, THE VELVET STONE CORAL OR VELVET LUMP CORAL. THEY REQUIRE 9 HOURS OF STRONG LIGHT PER DAY, MODERATE WATER MOVEMENT AND CAN TOLERATE NEIGHBORING FLOWER ANIMALS.

wart-like growths which may be white on a tan background. They prefer being planted in the soft sandy bottom of a mini-reef providing it gets enough light (7 hours per day minimum). It is a very fragile species with the fingers easily breaking off. The popular Velvet Fingers come in green, purple, yellow and tan.

Montipora digitata, the Velvet Finger Coral, with its polyps extended.

VELVET STONE, VELVET LUMP CORAL

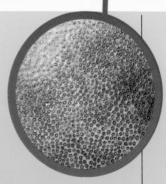

MONTIPORA SPONGODES
Bernard, 1897

This is really a well known false name because, while it assumes many shapes, none of the shapes of this species is like a velvet stone or lump. These are found from Japan to Australia and are finger-like more than anything else. The coral in the photograph requires 9 hours of direct light and moderate water agitation. The specimen shown is one of the types sold under this name.

Photo by Walt Deas.

ABOVE; *MONTIPORA VERRUCOSA*, THE VELVET CORAL, REQUIRES 9 HOURS
OF STRONG LIGHT WITH MODERATE WATER MOTION. IT IS NOT
AGGRESSIVE. BELOW: *MONTIPORA SPONGODES*, THE VELVET STONE
CORAL, REQUIRES 9 HOURS OF LIGHT AND MODERATE WATER MOVEMENT.
WHILE IT IS A DIFFICULT FLOWER ANIMAL TO MAINTAIN IN AN AQUARIUM,
IT FLOURISHES FOR SOME MINI-REEFERS WHO CAN'T EXPLAIN THE REASON
FOR THEIR SUCCESS.

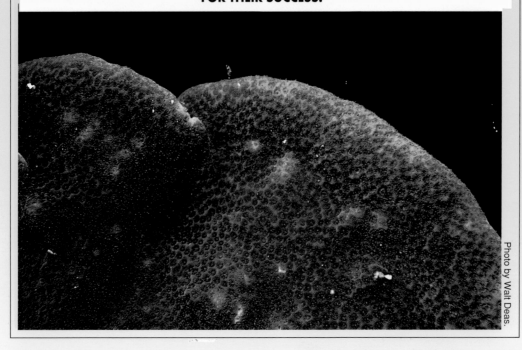

Photo by Walt Deas.

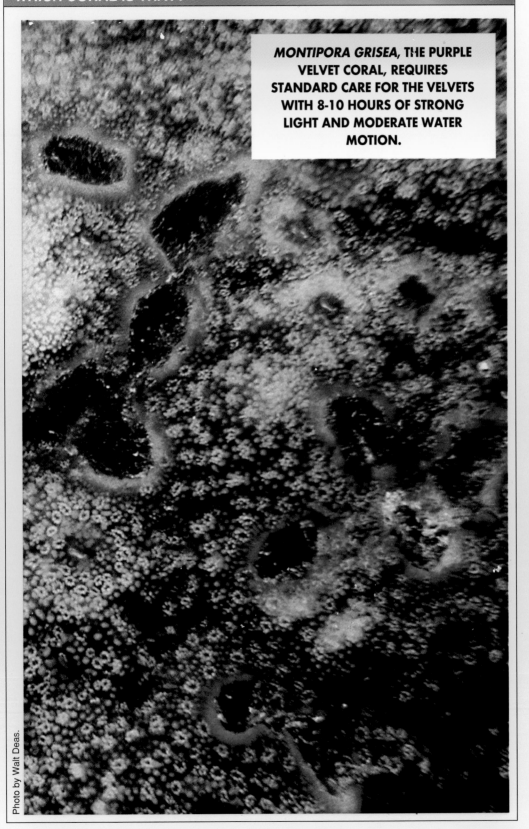

MONTIPORA GRISEA, THE PURPLE VELVET CORAL, REQUIRES STANDARD CARE FOR THE VELVETS WITH 8-10 HOURS OF STRONG LIGHT AND MODERATE WATER MOTION.

Photo by Walt Deas.

RUFFLED CORAL,
COLLAR CORAL

THE GENUS *MERULINA*
Ehrenberg, 1834

The derivation of the name is from two Latin words *merus* meaning *pure* and *linea* meaning line. If you examine the coral carefully, you'll find irregular mountains and valleys which extend from the center in a fan-shaped manner. The genus contains species which range from the Red Sea to Japan and Australia.

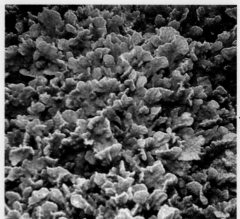

Merulina ampliata.

changes every two weeks. Needs trace elements.

MERULINA AMPLIATA, THE RUFFLED CORAL, REQUIRES TURBID WATER AND 8 HOURS OF DIRECT SUNLIGHT.

Photos by Dr. Elizabeth M. Wood.

RUFFLED CORAL

Merulina ampliata
Ellis & Solander, 1786

At night they are pretty and they are also plentiful throughout their range. During night dives, I often paused to *smell the roses* and appreciate their beauty. they need 8 hours of intense light, turbid water which is immaculately clean. Change the water every few months with 20%

COLLAR CORAL

MERULINA SCABRICULA
Dana, 1846

These can be beautiful in red, pink, yellow and green but they are extremely difficult to keep alive. They need 10 hours of intense light and moderate water movement. They are a lagoon species and enjoy slightly higher water temperatures of about 80°F.

Photo by Walt Deas.

ABOVE: *MERULINA SCABRICULA*, THE TAN RUFFLED CORAL, IS EXTREMELY DIFFICULT TO MAINTAIN UNLESS YOU GIVE IT 10 HOURS OF SUNLIGHT (OR ITS ARTIFICIAL EQUIVALENT) AND MODERATELY HEAVY WATER MOVEMENT. IT DOESN'T BOTHER OTHER FLOWER ANIMALS. BELOW: *MERULINA* SPECIES, SIMPLY CALLED MERULINA IN THE TRADE, REQUIRES THE SAME CARE AS *SCABRICULA*.

Photo by Walt Deas.

Photo by Dr. Elizabeth M. Wood.

SOLENASTREA BOURNONI, THE STARLET CORAL, IS THE MINI-REEFERS DREAM. IT IS BEAUTIFUL, HARDY, NOT FUSSY ABOUT LIGHTING WHICH CAN BE AS LOW AS TWO HOURS DAILY (THOUGH 8 HOURS IS BETTER), VERY MODERATE WATER MOVEMENT AND ONLY MODERATELY AGGRESSIVE. IT IS VERY SUITABLE FOR BEGINNERS.

STAR, STARLET CORAL

THE GENUS *SOLENASTREA*
Milne-Edwards & Haime, 1848

The name *Solenastrea* derives from the Greek *solen* which means *channel* and *aster* which means *star*. In nature it develops huge colonies which are either rounded or half-rounded. The corallites are isolated and very distinct both in the living and skeletal coralla. The basic colors are reddish brown and milky green. It is active at night because the polyps are retracted during the day. This species is almost always confused in the aquarium trade (and in aquarium books) with *Montastrea annularis* and especially *Stephanocoenia* and it

is impossible to differentiate them when living specimens are compared. There are two recognized species. *Solenastrea bournoni* Milne-Edwards & Haime has calices about 1/10 inch (2.0-2.5 mm) and its costae (that part of the septa which protrudes outside the corallite wall) are extended far outside the corallite wall. The other species, *hyades*, has calices which are larger, 3.0-3.5 mm (25.4 mm = one inch).

These are American species found in the Gulf of Mexico, the Florida Keys and most of the Caribbean Islands. They are plentiful in the aquarium trade from supplies shipped from Mexico. They are also collected in Florida north to the Carolinas. They are very easy to acclimate to the aquarium, without excessive lighting or water flow needs.

MONTASTREA ANNULARIS IS USUALLY MISTAKEN FOR SOLENASTREA BOURNONI IN THE TRADE, BUT IT DOESN'T MATTER SINCE BOTH ARE BEAUTIFUL AND BOTH ARE EASILY CARED FOR. LIGHT WATER MOTION AND 4-8 HOURS OF STRONG LIGHT.

Photo by Dr. Elizabeth M. Wood.

Jean Deas on the Great Barrier Reef helping to identify the photos in this book!

Photo by Walt Deas.

THE NON-SCLERACTINIAN CORALS

are the corals that (mostly) don't build reefs and are not hard.

They do not build skeletons of calcium carbonate (though a few do) and they might be Hydrozoans and not corals at all. They are very attractive and reasonably successful in the mini-reef aquarium.

In the early days of diving (1949-1970), I did not wear a so-called wet suit because they didn't exist at that time. I used a bathing suit and T-shirt top. Diving on reefs often included entering caves to find hidden fishes, lobsters (to eat!) and to satisfy my curiosity. Often, if not always, the roofs of these caves were covered with these animals. Most of them sting with a lingering burning sensation. I always carried Adolph's Meat Tenderizer which is derived from the juice of the papaya. Putting this liberally on my wounds, I was relieved of the burning and itching. (Thank you Dr. Leonard P. Schultz!).

PIPE ORGAN CORAL
THE GENUS *TUBIPORA*
Linnaeus, 1758

It has many commercial uses besides a decoration in the mini-reef aquarium. Its skeleton is completely pigmented, through and through, so that pieces retain their color and can be fashioned into ornaments. The name derives from the Latin with *tubus* meaning *tube*, of course; *porus* means *pore*.

TUBIPORA MUSICA, THE PIPE ORGAN CORAL, IS A DELIGHT IN THE AQUARIUM. IT IS EASY TO CARE FOR IF YOU GIVE IT LOTS OF LIGHT, PLENTY OF WATER MOVEMENT AND AN OCCASIONAL FEEDING OF NEWLY HATCHED BRINE SHRIMP.

Photo by Walt Deas.

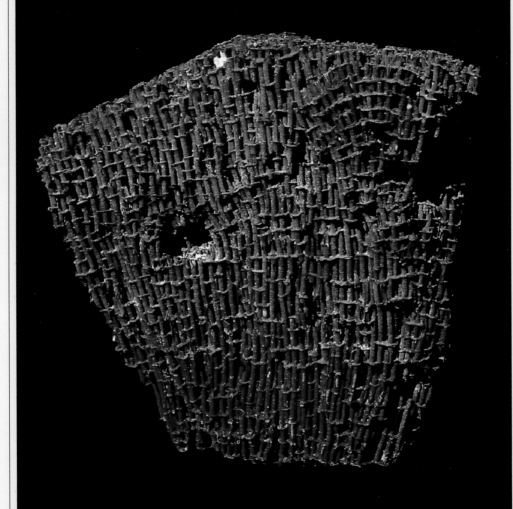

TUBIPORA MUSICA, THE PIPE ORGAN CORAL SKELETON. PHOTO BY DR. HERBERT R. AXELROD.

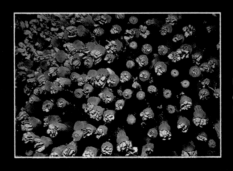

Unexpanded polyps of *Tubipora musica*. Photo by Walt deas.

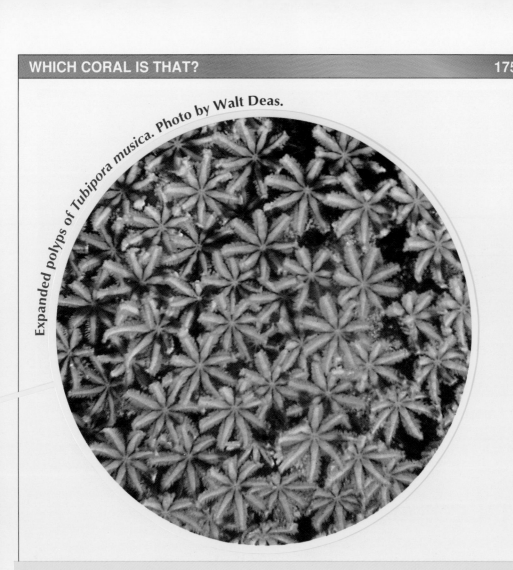

Expanded polyps of *Tubipora musica*. Photo by Walt Deas.

TUBIPORA MUSICA, THE PIPE ORGAN CORAL, REQUIRES HEAVY LIGHTING, HEAVY AERATION AND MODERATE SPACE.

TUBIPORA MUSICA
Linnaeus, 1758

This is a well known coral because the skeleton is sold as a curio. Once you see it, you'll never forget it. It is bright red and consists of a huge number of tubes bound together. Only the uppermost sections house polyps. Pieces broken off do well in the aquarium. The skeletons are red. The polyps vary in color. There are a dozen tubes to the inch. The polyps are very sensitive. When a brine shrimp touches them, they trap it and the entire ring of eight tentacles retracts. Can tolerate all lighting situations from 2 hours to 12 hours of strong light; it tolerates all water movements from slow to turbulent. It has a wide distribution from the Red Sea to the Marshall Islands. It is usually not seen by divers because its red skeleton is hidden by inconspicuous polyps. This is a rare non-scleractinian which has a calcareous skeleton.

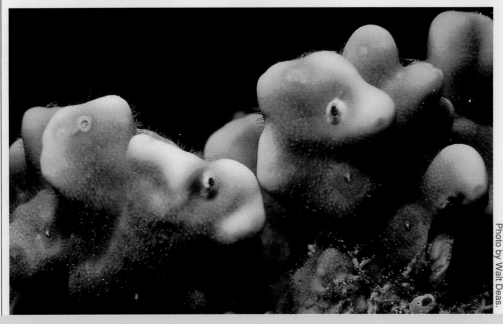

Photo by Walt Deas.

MILLEPORA ALCICORNIS, THE FIRE CORAL, HAS STINGING TENTACLES AND STINGING CELLS IN ITS POLYPS. IT REQUIRES AN EXPERIENCED AQUARIST TO KEEP IT ALIVE AND HEALTHY. IT NEEDS HEAVY LIGHTING, MODERATE TURBULENCE AND COMPLETE ISOLATION FROM OTHER CORALS. DON'T TOUCH THIS CORAL WITH YOUR BARE HANDS!

FIRE CORAL,
STINGING CORAL

THE GENUS *MILLEPORA*
Linnaeus, 1758

The name derives from the Latin *mille* meaning *thousand* and *porus* meaning *pore*. The colonies develop branches which may become fused. The tentacles are small bristles which are extended during the day; the whole outside skeleton is also covered with stinging cells and they should NEVER BE HANDLED. When dried, their surface reveals the thousands of tiny pores from which the scientific name derives. This family contains species which are larger and more stocky than *Stylaster* and *Distichopora* which look like *Millepora* in other respects.

There are more than 45 references to species in the literature but as early as 1898 S.J.Hickson wrote (*On the Species of the Genus* Millepora) that there is only one species.

FIRE CORAL,
STINGING CORAL

MILLEPORA ALCICORNIS
Linnaeus, 1758

This coral is found from the Red Sea to the tip of South Africa to Australia, Japan and the Marquesas. It appears in many colors but mainly in shades of yellow or light green. They are difficult to maintain in the aquarium and should really only be kept by themselves as they kill any corals with which they have an

MILLEPORA TENELLA, THE FIRE CORAL, IS NEITHER EASY NOR SAFE IN THE MINI-REEF AQUARIUM, BUT CHALLENGES ARE WHAT MAKES THE HOBBY SO INTERESTING. HEAVY LIGHTING, MODERATE WATER MOVEMENT AND ISOLATION BECAUSE IT KILLS ITS NEIGHBORING FLOWER ANIMALS.

Photo by Walt Deas.

Millepora tenella.

Photo by Walt Deas.

MILLEPORA PLATYPHYLLIA, THE PLATE FIRE CORAL, IS A NASTY ANIMAL THAT TRULY STINGS. IN THE MINI-REEF AQUARIUM IT REQUIRES SEPARATION FROM OTHER CORALS, MODERATE AERATION AND LOTS OF LIGHT.

encounter. They require a lot of light; minimum 8 hours of intense lighting per day. Small feedings are helpful (brine shrimp) but they also thrive on fish waste debris if they have piscine company in their mini-reef tank.

Australian guide books list many Australian species, but there is probably only one species in many shapes and sizes.

LACE CORAL
THE GENUS *STYLASTER*
Gray, 1847

The name derives from the Greek; *stylos* means *style* and *aster* means *star*.

There are more than 45 species known by name only (no skeleton remains to be studied). No modern scientist is working on this genus so we don't know much about their names. but they appear in many shapes, sizes and habitats. Every cave in the oceans of the world contains something like a *Stylaster*. They are even found in the Arctic and Antarctic!!! Tourists collect them because they are flat and dry into nice souvenirs even though they develop an offensive odor as the polyps rot. Some aquarists keep them alive nicely but they require very high grade artificial sea salt with as many trace

Photo by Walt Deas.

STYLASTER SPECIES REQUIRES NORMAL LIGHT, SLOW WATER MOVEMENTS AND IS HIGHLY TERRITORIAL SO KEEP IT ISOLATED. IT DOES NOT THRIVE UNDER MANY MINI-REEF SITUATIONS BUT IT IS WORTH A TRY.

elements as possible. Change 25% of the water every week if they are part of a massive mini-reef aquarium.

GLOWING EMBER CORAL

THE GENUS *DISTICHOPORA* LAMARCK, 1816

The name derives from the Greek *di* meaning *two* and *toichos* meaning *rows*; the Latin word *porus* means *pore*. This is a genus of branched corals which stay small, rarely growing higher than 5 inches. They are flat (good for tourists' souvenirs) and are found in many colors. Some specimens even have two colors at the same time! The pores from which

appears tiny white tentacles, are arranged uniformly on the branches. They are cave dwellers...and they have a mild sting.

There are 36 species known by their names only. Mostly the names merely indicate color or describe the species such as *Distichopora violacea* in a vividly violet fan, while *Distichopora irregularis* is a non-uniform, lumpy mass. Since they are cave dwellers they don't need much light; nor do they need a lot of light. But they do need monthly feeding of brine shrimp. They should be maintained in the mini-reef tank in as shady a spot as possible. As with all non-scleractinian corals (=hydrozoans), they are capable of killing their coral neighbors.

STYLASTER SPECIES WHICH NEEDS NORMAL LIGHTING, SLOW WATER MOVEMENTS AND ISOLATION. PHOTO BY WALT DEAS.

Photo by Scott Johnson.

Distichopora violacea from Eniwetok.

Photo by Walt Deas.

***DISTICHOPORA* SPECIES. A CAVE SPECIES THAT REQUIRES NORMAL ROOM LIGHTING, VERY LITTLE WATER MOVEMENT AND WEEKLY FEEDING OF MASHED BRINE SHRIMP.**

THE LEATHER CORALS AND SOFT CORALS

The Order Alcyonacea contains the leather and soft corals. The leather corals are the most popular coral animals to be kept in the mini-reef aquarium because they are the most hardy. They belong basically to the genus *Sarcophyton*. They almost always have ample symbiotic algae (zooxanthellae) so feeding is neither necessary nor desirable unless otherwise noted. They are found in the lagoons of most reefs where they are protected from the larger fishes and pounding surf. They tolerate most levels of light and they depend upon many of the trace elements normally found in sea salts, especially strontium and iodine. While they are easy to maintain, they are also dangerous to other corals when they shed.

The soft corals in this family are fairly difficult to identify but since only a dozen or so different species are involved, you can rely upon the photographs.

The corals of the genus *Sarcophyton* are extremely easy to maintain (but be careful of their shedding!). The *Cladiella* are relatively easy to keep, but more difficult than the *Sarcophyton*. The

Sinularia are highly recommended and are easy to keep in the mini-reef aquarium. Between all of these genera are 50 nice soft corals, so why look at *Dendronephthya* which is almost impossible to maintain alive for more than 6 months. Also in this order are the *Xenia* and *Anthelia*, which are best kept by experienced mini-reefers.

Soft corals, especially those in the genera *Lobophytum*, *Sarcophyton* and *Sinularia* seem to be attractive to snails and Doridacead nudibranchs (also called *dorids*). While the dorids don't actually attack the coral polyps like the snails do, they secrete a poison which kills fishes and corals kept in the same aquarium. This poison is their only means of defense.

Photo by Dr. Gerald R. Allen & Roger Steene.

ALCYONIUM SPECIES, THE ENCRUSTING SOFT CORAL, IS EASILY MAINTAINED WITH 6 HOURS OF LIGHT AND MODERATE WATER MOVEMENT. THIS SPECIES MAY BE *FULVUM*.

CHILI, YELLOW ENCRUSTING LEATHER CORAL

**THE FAMILY ALCYONIDAE
GENUS *ALCYONIUM*
Alcyonium fulvum Forskål**

This species requires normal lighting from 3 to 6 hours per day

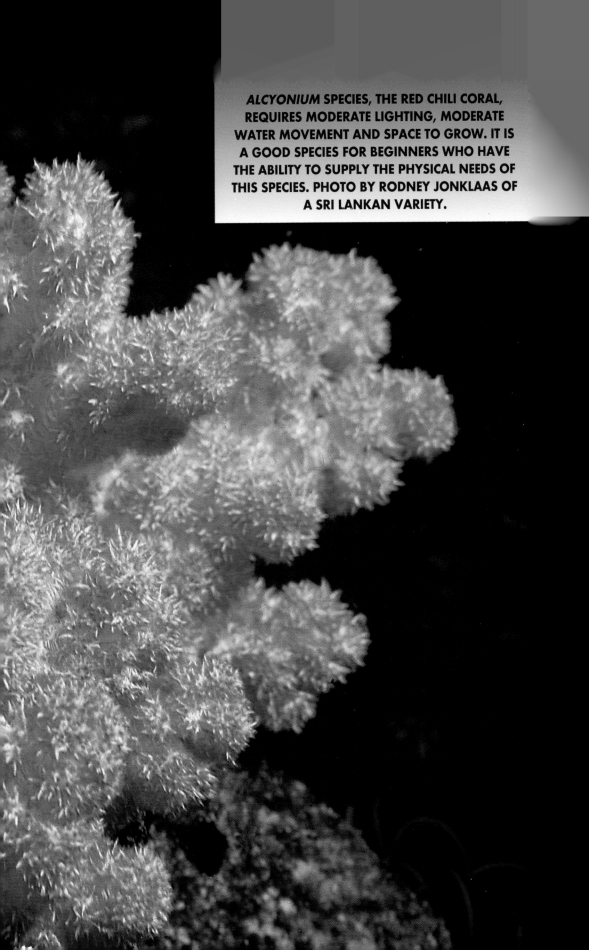

ALCYONIUM SPECIES, THE RED CHILI CORAL, REQUIRES MODERATE LIGHTING, MODERATE WATER MOVEMENT AND SPACE TO GROW. IT IS A GOOD SPECIES FOR BEGINNERS WHO HAVE THE ABILITY TO SUPPLY THE PHYSICAL NEEDS OF THIS SPECIES. PHOTO BY RODNEY JONKLAAS OF A SRI LANKAN VARIETY.

with light aeration (water movement). In its red form it has been called *chili coral* but the more usual colors are the tans and yellows. Many times this coral is imported as a gift on a piece of living rock where it might grow into a finger-shaped tree. The polyps sport star-burst shapes with 8 tentacles which grow from 1-2 inches in length. They should not be located closer than 5 inches to the next coral. Some nudibranchs attack them. I offer them newly hatched brine shrimp and they devour it; other mini-reefers are equally as successful without feeding but they have many fishes in with their corals.

LEATHER CORALS, TOADSTOOL CORALS

GENUS *SARCOPHYTON*

These are fast-growing corals which are typically found in shallow lagoons. Lagoons have three important characteristics: low water turbulence, good lighting and lots of food in the forms of single-celled algae and other small food animals which are supportive of rapid growth of the leather corals.

The *Sarcophyton* are terpenoidal. The terpenoids are toxins and are found in the skin of the leather corals, perhaps

SARCOPHYTON TROCHELIPHORUM, THE LEATHER CORAL, IS AN EASY CORAL FOR THE BEGINNER. IT REQUIRES ONLY 4 HOURS OF INTENSE LIGHT PER DAY AND LIGHT WATER MOVEMENTS. IT IS VERY AGGRESSIVE AND SHOULD NOT BE PLACED NEAR OTHER FLOWER ANIMALS.

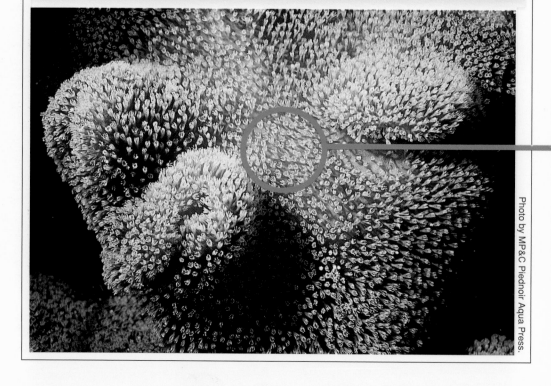

Photo by MP&C Piednoir Aqua Press.

protecting them from fishes (but not from nudibranchs).

They are all simple to care for requiring from 3-8 hours of strong light, feedings once a week (but not necessary if they are kept in with fishes), and lots of room so their terpenoids don't kill those corals adjacent to them.

Sarcophyton are easy to breed. Just cut them into pieces!

At times they seem to stop growing and appear diseased. This is a cleansing stage during which they will shed their outer covering. This outer covering is very toxic to fishes as well as other corals. When you see your leather coral falling back from perfect health, separate it into a hospital tank with very heavy aeration until the coat is shed. After shedding the coral animal looks much more beautiful than it did before the shedding. It is not unusual that they shed every week or two depending upon the cleanliness (turbidity) of your aquarium water. I have heard that some shed twice a week! Thin sheets of this shedding material usually kill whatever it lands on, so remove these shed skins if you can.

Most species like fluorescent lighting. Use as many white tubes as can fit into the top reflector, though at least one tube should be blue.

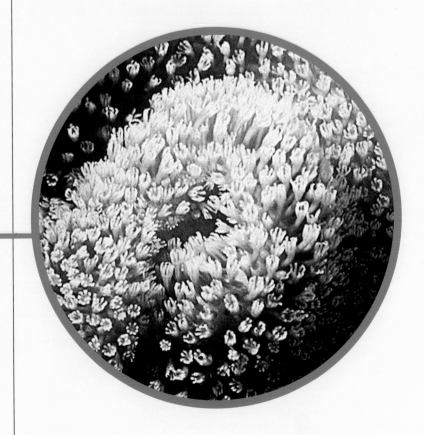

Photo by Walt Deas.

A fully grown *Sarcophyton trocheliphorum*.

LEATHER CORAL, TROUGH LEATHER, TOADSTOOL, MUSHROOM

SARCOPHYTON TROCHELIOPHORUM
Marenzeller

This well distributed leather coral ranges from the Red Sea throughout the Indian and Pacific Oceans. They can be found almost protruding from the water in shallow ebb pools during exceptionally low tides. Their colonies reach a yard in diameter. Cutting a piece from the growing edge of the coral and attaching it to a pieces of dead coral skeleton usually results in another *Sarcophyton*.

MUSHROOM LEATHER CORAL, GOLDEN CROWNED MUSHROOM

SARCOPHYTON ACUTANGULUM
Marenzeller

This leather coral came originally from the Red Sea exporters of tropical marine fishes, but now regular exports come from Africa, (mainly Mauritius and Kenya) as well as from Sri Lanka. These countries have no dependable protector of natural resources. They prefer moderately moving water, though their cuttings should be maintained in highly agitated

Photo by Dr. Gerald R. Allen and Roger Steene.

THE SOFT CORAL *SARCOPHYTON ACUTANGULUM*, THE MUSHROOM LEATHER CORAL, IS EASILY MAINTAINED WITH SLOWLY MOVING WATER AND 4 HOURS OF INTENSE LIGHT DAILY.

water. Most leather corals do better in agitated water, but they survive easily in moderate water flows.

They usually appear in tan colors but frequently are found in yellows and golds.

MUSHROOM CORAL, LEATHER CORAL

SARCOPHYTON LOBULATUM
Milne-Edwards & Haime

I have found the best specimens lying on the sand in less than one foot of water all around the Maldives Islands and Sri Lanka.

All *Sarcophyton* species require the same general care. Peter Wilkens and Johannes Birkholz describe their manner of propagating this species by cutting off 2-inch pieces from the base of the coral and fastening it to a piece of dead coral branch or mussel shell. They write that the wound will heal in two weeks and another colony will begin to develop. I have not had this same experience but, as always, we may have been dealing with two different corals since many of the *Sarcophyton* look alike.

SARCOPHYTON LOBULATUM, THE MUSHROOM CORAL, IS EASILY MAINTAINED WITH MODERATE WATER MOVEMENT AND 4-5 HOURS DAILY INTENSE LIGHTING. PHOTO BY WALT DEAS.

LEATHER, TROUGH LEATHER, TOADSTOOL CORAL

SARCOPHYTON MOLLE
Tixier Durivault

Here comes the danger! In general, *Sarcophyton* corals are ideal for most beginners. They are adaptable, inexpensive and hardy when given their minimal requirements. Then along comes an imitator which looks like *Sarcophyton irocheliophorum* but acts completely differently. *S. molle* is sold as though it were *S. trocheliophorum* but once in your aquarium you will notice it doesn't shed its skin. Instead it converges on itself and oozes large amount of mucus which does not quickly disperse. It can easily poison fish and other invertebrates in the aquarium. This is a very soft coral to the touch and for some reason it confuses anemone fishes, *Amphiprion*, to adopt it as their protector.

GOLDEN CROWN TOADSTOOL, MUSHROOM, LEATHER CORAL

SARCOPHYTON GLAUCUM
Quoy & Gaimard

This coral is very popular and is raised by farmers for aquarium purposes. It is readily acclimated to the mini-reef aquarium and is easily propagated by cutting off the head, leaving only the

SARCOPHYTON MOLLE IS EASILY MAINTAINED WITH MODERATE WATER FLOW AND 4 HOURS OF DIRECT INTENSE LIGHT. PHOTO BY WALT DEAS.

remaining stem (think of a mushroom). The head should have about a one inch piece of the stem. It can be attached to a solid base or simply planted in the sand. In a month or so it will open up and be amazingly beautiful. The remaining stem takes about two months to develop into its former beauty. This coral appears in many colors. Though the usual color of all *Sarcophyton* is tan, this species occurs in golden yellow, light and dark green.

This coral is famous in the world of toxicology because of the toxins it contains. The toxins are called *sarcophines* (derived from the genus name *Sarcophyton*).

EHRENBERG'S MUSHROOM, WHITE FAIRY, LEATHER TOADSTOOL

SARCOPHYTON EHRENBERGI
Marenzeller

This coral might very well be the best of the leather corals for the mini-reefer. It certainly is the most beautiful. It also is very available since it is found throughout the Red Sea and the Indian and tropical Pacific Oceans. It has wonderful, isolated 8-pronged tentacles, just like a miniature daisy flower. They adjust well in the mini-reef aquarium and should

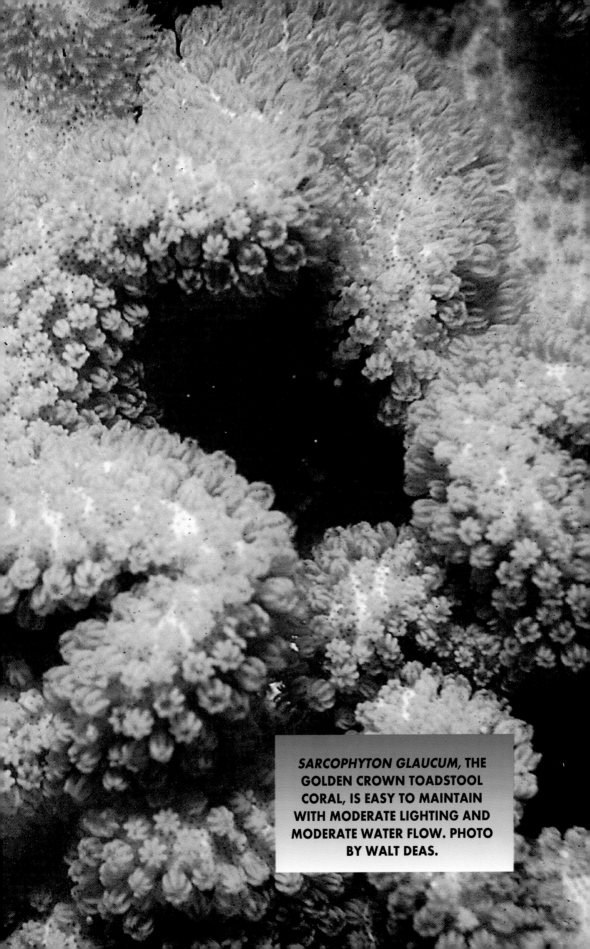

SARCOPHYTON GLAUCUM, THE GOLDEN CROWN TOADSTOOL CORAL, IS EASY TO MAINTAIN WITH MODERATE LIGHTING AND MODERATE WATER FLOW. PHOTO BY WALT DEAS.

Photo by Dr. Elizabeth M. Wood.

SARCOPHYTON EHRENBERGI, EHRENBERG'S MUSHROOM CORAL, IS SIMPLE TO MAINTAIN WITH MODERATE LIGHT AND WATER FLOW.

be offered newly hatched brine shrimp once their polyps are open and their tentacles are extended. If the environment is to its liking, this species never (or almost never) sheds its mucous coating. But even when it does shed, it rarely sheds more than twice a month and announces its shedding by retracting for a few days prior to shedding. This is a very sensitive coral and any stinging coral placed near it will certainly kill it if it can touch it with its stinging tentacles.

We have discussed the special *Sarcophyton* corals and their needs. Other *Sarcophyton* corals are illustrated and their needs are the same as described for the genus.

FLOWER LEATHER, CABBAGE, LETTUCE, FINGER

THE GENUS *LOBOPHYTUM*

Another member of the Alcyonidae is the genus *Lobophytum*. These corals look like *Sarcophyton* which are closed up. Many leather corals are imported without any scientific identifications. As one area (for example the Caribbean, Brazil, Cuba, Red Sea, etc.) becomes off-limits for collecting living rocks and other coral constituents,

LOBOPHYTON PAUCIFLORUM, **THE CABBAGE CORAL, IS FOR BEGINNERS WITH A MINIMUM OF 3 HOURS INTENSE LIGHTING PER DAY AND SLOW TO MODERATE WATER FLOWS. PHOTO BY WALT DEAS.**

other areas open up. This is especially true of the emerging Third World countries which are forced to do everything they can to bring in money by exporting natural resources which are replenishible. Many of these leather corals are unidentified but the trade gives them common names and some dealers often attribute scientific names based upon their similarity to well known corals which are illustrated in a book.

The *Lobophytum* are mainly encrusting species. They grow like grass rather than like trees. Keep this in mind when designing your

LOBOPHYTON CRASSUM, THE FLOWER LEATHER CORAL, HAS MINIMUM NEEDS OF 3 HOURS OF INTENSE, DIRECT LIGHT AND SLOW-MOVING WATERS BATHING IT. PHOTO BY WALT DEAS.

mini-reel aquarium. They release their waxy skin coat on a schedule of every 3-7 days, just like *Sarcophyton*. Their basic care is exactly the same as *Sarcophyton* in the aquarium.

CHRISTMAS TREE,
MEDUSA, POTATO

THE GENUS *SPHAERELLA*

Basically only one species is imported, namely, *Sphaerella krempfi* Hickson. This is a beautiful coral with the ability to contract until it looks like a tufted potato. They do not have symbiotic algae thus have no strong requirements for light. They are easily maintained with newly hatched brine shrimp. The shrimp should be offered only when their tentacles are extended. They are extremely sensitive to the nibbling of larger fishes.

Their basic care is the same as *Sarcophyton*.

CAROTALCYON SAGAMIANUM, THE CARROT-LEATHER CORAL REQUIRES MODERATE WATER FLOWS AND ROOM LIGHT. THEY HAVE NO ZOOXANTHELLAE TO WORRY ABOUT!

Photo by Peter Wilkens.

CARROT-LEATHER CORAL

THE GENUS *CAROTALCYON*

These corals are called *carrots* because they have the basic orange/red carrot color. Sometimes their basic color becomes blood red and they are gorgeous. They are heavy eaters and must be fed with newly hatched brine shrimp every few days. Their basic care is different than *Sarcophyton* as they need highly agitated water and constant feedings. They are not for beginners and even with the best of care they usually live less than one year. They do not contain symbiotic algae thus have no lighting requirements. They are edible for crabs, snails and coral-eating fishes like the parrot fishes.

SPHAERELLA KREMPFI, THE MEDUSA TREE CORAL, NEEDS A FEW HOURS OF INTENSE LIGHTING AND MODERATE WATER CURRENTS. IT IS NOT AGGRESSIVE. PHOTO BY DR. HERBERT R. AXELROD.

SPHAERELLA KREMPFI, THE MEDUSA TREE CORAL, IS GORGEOUS BUT NEEDS A FEW HOURS OF DIRECT STRONG LIGHTING AND MODERATE WATER MOVEMENT. PHOTO BY U. ERICH FRIESE.

SINULARIA SPECIES ARE DIFFICULT TO IDENTIFY. THESE TWO SPECIES OF *SINULARIA* ARE SIMPLE TO CARE FOR IN THE MINI-REEF AQUARIUM. THEY NEED 4-6 HOURS OF LIGHT AND STRONG WATER MOVEMENT.

Photos by U.Erich Friese

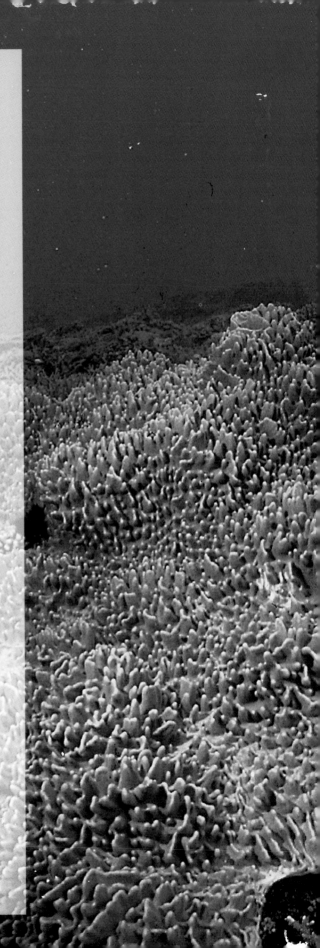

FINGER CORALS, FINGERED LEATHER CORALS
THE GENUS *SINULARIA*

These can be very easy to care for if their basic requirements are met. They have thick bases from which secondary branches under two inches in length project. They shed their skin once or twice a week and do not appreciate strong (halogen) lighting. Most species are tan colored and basically small (about 6 inches).

When they are open they should be fed. Be careful with the feeding unless there are small fishes which will eat the uneaten brine shrimp. There is more of a danger of over feeding, thus pollution, than in under feeding. Several authors report soaking their food in a general vitamin preparation. Ask your local pet shop which vitamins are preferred. I have used a general vitamin mixture available from the local health food store.

SINULARIA SPECIES, THE PURPLE FINGERS, IS AN EASY CORAL TO MAINTAIN. IT REQUIRES 6 HOURS OF LIGHT AND A HIGH VOLUME OF WATER PASSING AROUND IT.
PHOTO BY WALT DEAS.

Photo by Walt Deas.

SINULARIA MACROPODIA, THE GOLD FINGER CORAL, REQUIRES LITTLE CARE OTHER THAN 4-6 HOURS OF INTENSE LIGHTING AND MODERATE WATER MOVEMENT.

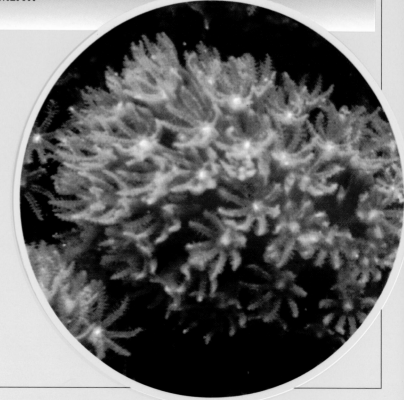

Photo by Walt Deas.

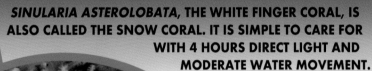

SINULARIA ASTEROLOBATA, **THE WHITE FINGER CORAL, IS ALSO CALLED THE SNOW CORAL. IT IS SIMPLE TO CARE FOR WITH 4 HOURS DIRECT LIGHT AND MODERATE WATER MOVEMENT.**

BUSH CORAL,
TREE CORAL

THE FAMILY NEPHTHEIDAE

These corals are colorful and are found in the areas on coral reefs where the seas are turbulent. They are found in all habitats from the stony bases to soft or coarse sand. The species usually imported is *Litophyton arboreum*. It comes from Indonesia and, if smaller specimens are flown in, are usually very hardy. Their main problem is parasites. Unlike most Nephtheidae, this species has zooxanthellae (symbiotic algae). The best way to treat *Litophyton* is to cut away all damaged or rotten segments. The cleansed piece should then be securely anchored so that a constant jet stream of filtered water is directed at it for a week. They usually secure themselves to the base upon which they were anchored.

They should be fed every few days with some newly hatched brine shrimp, *Artemia salina*.

The parasites are flat worms and it isn't clear whether they feed on the host itself or on the slime coating which is periodically shed. I have seen cases where the coral would be completely covered with flat worms and the host would die from lack of light. Every coral should be sterilized before being placed into the mini-reef aquarium. Sterilization takes place when a container of fresh water at the same pH and temperature as the mini-reef

aquarium is used to dip the coral in for a very short period of time. I count to ten (about 5 seconds), shaking the coral violently while it is in the freshwater bath.

NEPHTHEA SPECIES, A TREE CORAL, REQUIRES LIGHT BECAUSE IT CONTAINS ZOOXANTHELLAE, 6 HOURS A DAY WITH MODERATE WATER MOVEMENT. IT SHOULD ALSO BE FED ONCE A WEEK WITH NEWLY HATCHED BRINE SHRIMP. PHOTO BY MP&C PIEDNOIR AQUA PRESS.

Some fishes eat flat worms when they are hungry. But usually fishes in the mini-reef aquarium are well fed. What fish doesn't like to eat worms?

COLT CORALS

THE GENUS *CLADIELLA*

Like most genera of corals, the various members may take on different shapes and colors. *Cladiella* is no exception. This is a genus of attractive corals which often appears in orange to brown. They are very hardy and are highly recommended for the beginner. One of the problems for the beginner is to be sure it is a *Cladiella* which was acquired and not a similar looking species.

Feeding is done with the usual newly hatched brine shrimp nauplii when the polyps and tentacles are extended.

Reproduction is by cutting, though more elaborate methods are used commercially. They prefer a medium amount of light. That given off by 4 white fluorescent tubes, perhaps with a blue tube added, is enough. Halogen light must be GRADUALLY introduced. *Cladiella* has strong stinging tentacles and quickly destroys any adjacent *Sinularia* or *Sarcophyton* corals with which they make contact.

With all corals, regardless of genera, they do best when they have plenty of room between them and the next living flower animal. Small fishes are fine but many invertebrates like worms, snails, and crabs and large fishes attack the soft corals (including the leather corals) and kill them.

THE TWO PHOTOS, ABOVE AND BELOW, SHOW THE COLT CORAL, *CLADIELLA*, IN POOR CONDITION AFTER JUST ARRIVING IN A SHIPMENT.

Photo by Dr. Herbert R. Axelrod.

CLADIELLA SPECIES ARE CALLED COLT CORAL. THEY ARE EXCELLENT FOR STARTING MINI-REEFERS. THEY MAY WELL BE ONE OF THE MOST ACCOMMODATING OF THE CORALS BUT THEY ARE VERY DIFFICULT TO IDENTIFY. IT DOESN'T MATTER, THEY ARE ALL THE SAME AS FAR AS CARE IS CONCERNED. LIGHTING IS NOT IMPORTANT, THEY ARE ALSO NOT FUSSY ABOUT WATER MOVEMENT AND THEY CAN TOLERATE LITTLE OR A LOT OF WATER MOTION. BELOW IS A COLT CORAL THRIVING IN A HOME AQUARIUM.

Photo by Glen S. Axelrod.

CARNATION CORALS,
CHRISTMAS TREES

THE GENUS *DENDRONEPHTHYA*

If you are a beginner, skip this genus and come back in six months. These corals are difficult even for the professionals, that's why you see them so infrequently. Yet, because of their beauty and the fact that they take so long to die, they are shipped out of the usual areas in the Indo-Pacific from which coral reef fishes are exported. Regardless of what other books claim, these corals must have heavy aeration by means of a constant strong current. Additionally, they must have agitated strong current twice a day to basically imitate the tides in their natural habitat. They also must be fed several times daily with newly hatched brine shrimp. They don't require much light; 8 hours with two white fluorescents is sufficient. Their mini-reef aquarium should be free of fishes and other living things because the violent water will make their short lives miserable as they stay in a corner where the current isn't too strong. Experts have used sponges, mussels and tube worms as companions in the mini-reef with *Dendronephthya*. If you have any success at all with these corals you should report it to the magazine *TROPICAL FISH HOBBYIST* (the same company that published this book), so other mini-reefers can be enriched by your experiences.

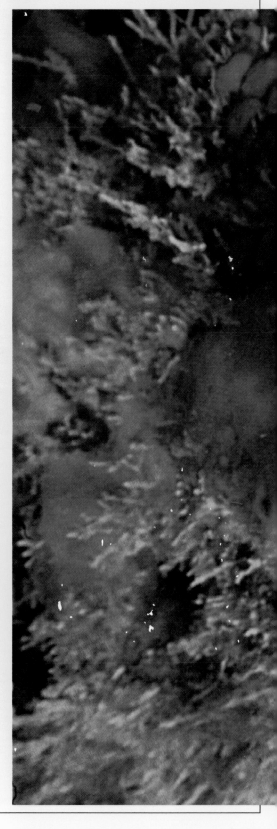

DENDRONEPHTHYA AUREA, THE GOLD CARNATION, IS NOT FOR BEGINNERS. THEY REQUIRE LITTLE LIGHT AND NOT MUCH OF A WATER FLOW BUT THEY RARELY LIVE FOR A YEAR IN THE AVERAGE WELL-MANAGED MINI-REEF AQUARIUM.

Photo by Walt Deas.

DENDRONEPHTHYA MIRABELIS, THE WHITE CARNATION CORAL, REQUIRES ROOM LIGHT BECAUSE THEY DO NOT CONTAIN ZOOXANTHELLAE (SYMBIOTIC ALGAE), A MODERATE WATER MOVEMENT AND CAN BE POSITIONED CLOSE TO OTHER FLOWER ANIMALS.

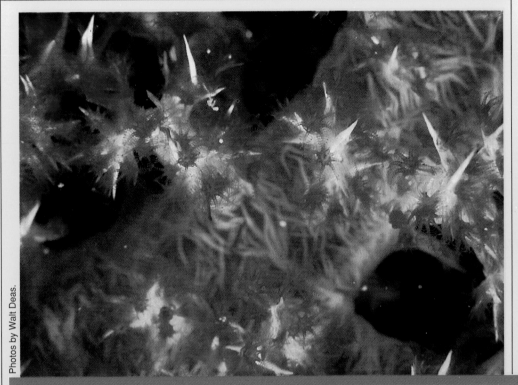

Photos by Walt Deas.

DENDRONEPHTHYA SPECIES, THE SPIKE CARNATION ABOVE, AND *DENDRONEPHTHYA* SPECIES, THE PURPLE CARNATION SHOWN BELOW, REQUIRE LITTLE LIGHT, MODERATE WATER MOVEMENT AND WEEKLY FEEDINGS OF MASHED BRINE SHRIMP.

DENDRONEPHTHYA SPECIES, THE VIOLACEOUS CARNATION, DOES NOT REQUIRE SPECIAL LIGHTING AS IT DOES NOT CONTAIN SYMBIOTIC ALGAE (ZOOXANTHELLAE). LIGHT WATER MOVEMENT AND WEEKLY FEEDINGS ARE REQUIRED, BUT IT IS STILL HARD TO MAINTAIN SUCCESSFULLY. PHOTO BY WALT DEAS.

DENDRONEPHTHYA SPECIES, ALSO CALLED THE PINK CARNATION AS SOME THREE OTHER SPECIES ARE, HAS LITTLE LIGHT REQUIREMENTS AS IT DOES NOT CONTAIN SYMBIOTIC ALGAE. MODERATE WATER MOVEMENT IS APPRECIATED. PHOTO BY WALT DEAS.

Photos by Walt Deas.

TWO *DENDRONEPHTHYA* SPECIES. THE PHOTO ABOVE SHOWS THE GOLDEN CARNATION WHILE THE LOWER PHOTO SHOWS THE BLOOD RED CARNATION. BOTH ARE DIFFICULT TO MAINTAIN. BUT THEY THRIVE IN LOW LIGHTING SITUATIONS WITH MODERATE WATER MOVEMENT.

JEAN DEAS WITH A BLOOD RED CARNATION, *DENDRONEPHTHYA*. THIS PHOTO GIVES SOME IDEA OF THE SIZE THESE ANIMALS REACH. PHOTO BY WALT DEAS.

Photos by Walt Deas.

PARALEMNALIA SPECIES SHOWN ABOVE IS CALLED THE BROWN CARNATION AND *SCLERONEPHTHYA* SPECIES SHOWN BELOW IS KNOWN AS THE ORANGE CARNATION. BOTH DO NOT CONTAIN ALGAE SO THEY HAVE NO REAL NEED FOR BRIGHT LIGHTING. THEY ARE FOND OF MODERATELY MOVING WATER BUT STILL ARE NOT FOR BEGINNING MINI-REEFERS.

SCLERONEPHTHYA SPECIES, THE WARTY SOFT CORAL, CONTAINS NO SYMBIOTIC ALGAE THEREFORE DOES NOT REQUIRE BRIGHT LIGHTING. IT THRIVES UNDER MODERATE WATER MOVEMENT AND WEEKLY FEEDINGS OF NEWLY HATCHED BRINE SHRIMP. PHOTO BY WALT DEAS.

PULSING CORAL,
WAVING CORAL

THE FAMILY XENIIDAE
Ehrenberg 1828

Keeping any corals in your mini-reef aquarium creates problems. Most of the corals kept in mini-reef aquariums are fixed and barely move. Their movements are usually growth movements which are imperceptible over the short haul. There are, however, corals which move. These corals, commonly called *pulsing* or *waving* corals, are very interesting for the aquarium because they move. Why they move is not very clear. The accepted theories are hardly convincing. The modern idea of why the xeniids move is to remove gases and water from the animal. The xeniids have such a massive surface area with their extended polyps and tentacles that it is difficult to imagine this to be true. It has been shown that these pulsating movements are not for the purpose of catching foods because they have been maintained for years without feeding. The family contains three genera which are of interest to mini-reefers, namely, *Xenia*, *Anthelia* and *Cespitularia*.

The individual polyps of all the xeniids may reach more than half inch in length. All contain symbiotic algae so their basic color is tan, though there are some exceptions, especially those xeniids which are found in very clear, shallow water where the

A MAGNIFICENT UNDERWATER SCENE SHOWING *XENIA* PULSING CORALS IN THE PHILIPPINE ISLANDS. THESE REQUIRE SUBSTANTIAL WATER MOVEMENT, 8 HOURS OR SO OF INTENSE LIGHTING AND THEY CAN BE LOCATED CLOSE TO OTHER FLOWER ANIMALS. PHOTO BY MP&C PIEDNOIR AQUA PRESS.

Photo by Dr. L.P.Zann.

CESPITULARIA, THE OCTOPUS CORAL, SPECIES HAVE EIGHT TENTACLES AND SOMETIMES THEY PULSE. THEY ARE NOT DIFFICULT TO MAINTAIN IF THE SPECIMEN HAS NOT BE DAMAGED IN TRANSIT. THEY REQUIRE 8 HOURS OF INTENSE LIGHT PER DAY, HIGH WATER MOVEMENT AND SOME SPACE TO GROW.

XENIA SPECIES, THE TABBY PULSING CORAL, REQUIRES HEAVY WATER MOVEMENT AND SUBSTANTIAL LIGHTING AT LEAST 8 HOURS PER DAY.

Photo by Walt Deas.

sun exposure forces them to develop anti-UV pigments. These pigments may be red, green or blue, or combinations thereof.

POM-PON, PULSING CORALS, FEATHER CORAL

THE GENUS *XENIA*

This is a generously populated genus. Many common names are attached based upon the shape and color of the individual coral. This only causes confusion. These animals need a strong current but

Photo by Walt Deas.

XENIA UMBELLATA, THE UMBRELLA XENIA, IS THE PRETTIEST OF THE XENIA. IT NEEDS HEAVY WATER MOVEMENT AND INTENSE LIGHTING FOR 9 HOURS PER DAY.

UMBRELLA, GLOVE XENIA, MUSHROOM

XENIA UMBELLATA

This species was selected from the genus because it is the prettiest of the genus. It has a definite mushroom shape and is rarely seen in good health because they are so abused in shipping. You should only acquire *umbellata* when they can be seen alive in a mini-reef environment. They do best with halogen lights to which they have gradually

when the current is too strong they no longer pulsate. As a matter of fact, many usually stop pulsating after they have become established in the mini-reef. *Xenia* are corals for the experienced mini-reefer, DEFINITELY NOT FOR THE BEGINNER. These do not have to be fed and, in fact, do best in nutrient poor water. We don't know much about them, obviously.

become accustomed. Don't be upset if they stop pulsing. They are easily attacked by aggressive fishes and they stop pulsing when this happens. They are best when kept alone but that is not the purpose of a mini-reef aquarium. They reproduce by shedding living planula larvae. They are a challenge to maintain and only experts can keep them alive for a year or more. It seems their longevity depends upon their being pampered, though they live if protected from predatory snails, fishes and worms.

CLOSELY RELATED TO THE FAMILIAR *XENIA* IS THE *HETEROXENIA* SPECIES CALLED THE FALSE XENIA CORAL, THEY ARE EASIER TO MAINTAIN THAN *XENIA*. THEY NEED 8 HOURS INTENSE LIGHTING, HEAVY WATER MOVEMENTS AND CAN BE CROWDED.

Photo by Walt Deas.

Photo by Walt Deas.

MINABAE ALDERSLADEI, SOMETIMES REFERRED TO AS THE POM-PON XENIA, HAS THE SAME REQUIREMENTS AS *HETEROXENIA.* THE SCIENTIFIC NAME OF THIS SPECIES HAS NOT BEEN CONFIRMED BUT WAS SUPPLIED BY THE PHOTOGRAPHER. IN ANY CASE, IT IS CLOSELY RELATED TO *XENIA.*

XENIA PUERTOGALERAE, THE WEDDING VEIL XENIA, REQUIRES 8 HOURS OF DIRECT LIGHTING AND HEAVY WATER MOVEMENT TO THRIVE. PHOTO BY WALT DEAS.

Xenia elongata. Photo by Keith Gillette.

Photo by Dr. Leon P. Zann.

ANTHELIA GLAUCA, THE GIANT ANTHELIA, REQUIRES 9 HOURS OF INTENSE LIGHTING AND HEAVY WATER MOVEMENT.

WAVING CORALS, ANTHELIA

THE GENUS *ANTHELIA*

These corals are not as difficult to maintain as some of the other, more delicate species of xeniid corals. They rhythmically open and close every few seconds as though they were trying to trap food, attract attention or just flexing their muscles. No one knows for sure why they have this behavior except we know it is not for feeding. They do not tolerate close association with other soft or leather corals. With dozens of species (or varieties) being imported, identification is difficult, but it doesn't really matter which species is which as long as you can recognize the genus to which they belong. The most commonly imported species is *Anthelia glauca*. This is called the giant anthelia because it has polyps that grow several inches and they open and close every two or three seconds. They are desirable foods for some fishes, especially tangs, so they do best in tanks without fishes. They have the telltale 8 leafed tentacles which give this coral (and the rest of the genus) a bushy appearance. They are all attacked by fishes, worms, snails and other, more aggressive flower animals.

Photo by Dr. Leon P. Zann.

ANTHELIA SPECIES, THE WAVING HAND CORAL, REQUIRES 8 HOURS OF INTENSE LIGHTING PER DAY WITH ACTIVELY MOVING WATER.

ENCRUSTING ANEMONES, BUTTON POLYPS, SEA MATS

THE ORDER ZOANTHINIARIA

This large group of more than 285 species are small six-tentacled (or multiples of six) coral-like animals. They rarely reach an inch in diameter, but they colonize and can become quite large. Reproduction is by budding. These animals have no skeleton but do develop a tough skin in which all kinds of debris are trapped including sand, bits of shells, etc. They have stinging capacity but it is not strong. They require feeding of live brine shrimp, even week old shrimp are taken. They are simple to care for

ZOANTHUS SPECIES, THE GOLDEN BUTTON CORAL, ARE HIGHLY RECOMMENDED FOR BEGINNERS. THEY HAVE MINIMAL LIGHTING NEEDS AND 3 HOURS OF INTENSE LIGHTING PER DAY IS SUFFICIENT. MODERATE WATER MOVEMENT AND LITTLE GROWING SPACE ROUNDS OUT THEIR NEEDS.

and are highly recommended for the beginner. They adjust to most light conditions and should be maintained only in quality artificial salt water made with plenty of trace elements. They thrive when they are properly fed and have enough iodine. I use iodized salt, sold for human consumption, as a weekly additive after properly calculating the specific gravity of the water already in the mini-reef aquarium.

The two most interesting genera for mini-reefers are the genera *Zoanthus* and *Palythoa*. It is often extremely difficult to differentiate between these two genera except for a close scrutiny of the accompanying photographs. They all require the same care with a gentle water flow, any kind of lighting, and constant feeding. Keep them free of predators.

STAR POLYPS, PIPE CORALS, EIGHT TENTACLED ANTHOZOANS

THE GENUS *CLAVULARIA*

If there is such a thing as grass growing in a mini-reef aquarium, this is it. From an unpaved mat of very strong, flexible material up grows star polyps of many colors, depending upon the species. This base grows slowly but steadily, overcoming all minor obstacles in its path. If there is a shell or ornament in its way, it just grows over it. During all of this growth it keeps sprouting polyps which are so dense they look like coarse grasses. All of them are easy to keep and are strongly recommended for the beginning

PALYTHOA SPECIES, THE GREEN MOON POLYP CORAL, IS EASY TO CARE FOR WITH 5 HOURS INTENSE LIGHTING, MODERATE WATER MOTION AND SOME ROOM TO GROW.

Photo by U. Erich Friese.

CARIJOA SPECIES, THE STICK POLYP CORAL, DOES FAIRLY WELL ON 6 HOURS INTENSE LIGHTING AND MODERATE WATER MOVEMENT. THESE CORALS BELONG TO THE FAMILY CLAVULARIIDAE.

Photo by Walt Deas.

Photo by U. Erich Friese.

ABOVE: *ZOANTHUS* SPECIES, THE OLIVE ENCRUSTING CORAL, NEEDS LITTLE LIGHT (2 HOURS PER DAY OF INTENSE LIGHTING) AND MODERATE WATER MOTION. BELOW: *PALYTHOA*, THE GREEN SEA MAT CORAL, REQUIRES 4 HOURS OF DIRECT INTENSE LIGHT, MODERATE WATER MOTION AND LITTLE ROOM FOR GROWTH.

Photo by U. Erich Friese.

Photo by U. erich Friese.

ABOVE: *ZOANTHUS* SPECIES, THE GOLDEN SEA MAT CORAL, IS EASILY CARED FOR IN THE MINI-REEF AQUARIUM. IT REQUIRES 3 HOURS OF INTENSE LIGHT AND A MODERATE FLOW OF WATER AROUND IT. BELOW: *ZOANTHUS PULCHELLUS*, THE GREEN BUTTON SEA MAT, IS IDEAL FOR THE BEGINNER. ONLY 2 HOURS OF INTENSE LIGHTING, MODERATE WATER MOVEMENT AND NOT TOO MUCH SPACE ARE THE REQUIREMENTS. I'VE NEVER SEEN THIS SPECIES FAIL IN THE MINI-REEF TANK IF THESE PHYSICAL CONDITIONS ARE SUPPLIED. THIS SPECIES HAS ALSO BEEN PLACED IN THE GENUS *PALYTHOA*.

Photo by U. Erich Friese.

ZOANTHUS SPECIES, THE LONG-HAIRED SEA MAT, IS EASY TO CARE FOR. JUST 2 HOURS OF INTENSE LIGHTING PER DAY AND MODERATE WATER MOVEMENT ARE REQUIRED. PHOTO BY MP&C PIEDNOIR AQUA PRESS.

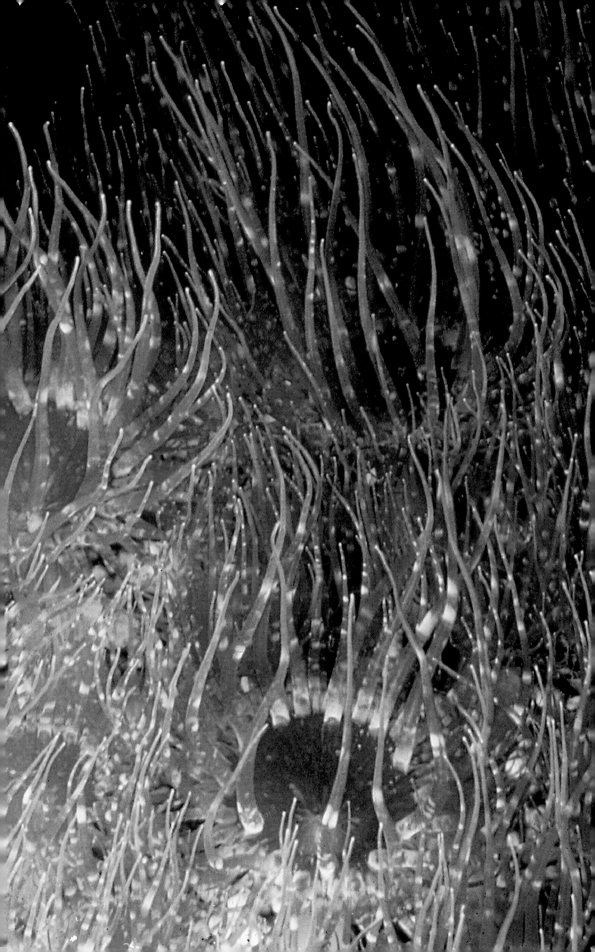

Photo by U. Erich Friese.

ABOVE: *PARAZOANTHUS GRACILIS,* THE BALLET DANCER CORAL, IS NOT DIFFICULT TO CARE FOR. IT REQUIRES 3-4 HOURS OF DIRECT, INTENSE LIGHTING PER DAY PLUS MODERATE WATER MOTION THROUGH ITS TENTACLES. BELOW: *TELESTO* SPECIES, THE OCTOCORAL, REQUIRES 3 HOURS OF INTENSE LIGHTING AND ROOM TO GROW AS IT IS A FAST GROWER UNDER IDEAL CONDITIONS.

CLAVULARIA VIRIDIS, THE GREEN STAR POLYPS CORAL, IS SIMPLE TO CARE FOR WITH 5 HOURS OF INTENSE LIGHTING AND A MODERATE FLOW OF WATER OVER THE ENTIRE FLOWER ANIMAL. PHOTO BY MP&C PIEDNOIR AQUA PRESS.

Photo by Walt Deas.

CARIJOA SPECIES, THE BLUSHING STICK POLYP CORAL, REQUIRES 8 HOURS OF INTENSE LIGHTING, MODERATE WATER MOTION AND SOME GROWING SPACE.

mini-reefer. They need minimum light but they also get along with strong light. A gentle flow of water is highly recommended. Because they contain symbiotic algae (zooxanthellae) they do not require feeding. They are usually attacked by reef fishes.

They reproduce like grass. Cut off a piece and plant it anywhere and it usually grows. They need calcium fertilization by means of calcium water to assist them in growth, but they grow so quickly that this fertilization may not be necessary.

CARIJOA SPECIES, THE CHRISTMAS TREE POLYP CORAL, A MEMBER OF THE FAMILY CLAVULARIIDAE, REQUIRES 8 HOURS OF INTENSE LIGHT PER DAY AND MODERATE WATER MOVEMENT.

Photo by Walt Deas.

Diver Peter Allen gives you some idea of the size to which Melithaeidae, gorgonian fans, grows. Photo by Walt Deas.

THE GORGONIANS,
FAN CORALS

ORDER: GORGONIACEA

The tropical seas and oceans of the world are laden with gorgonians of all types. So complex is the taxonomy of these organisms that few scientists are regularly studying them. This leaves the mini-reefer with few reliable choices as far as nomenclature is concerned.

Gorgonians are the cheapest of the so-called corals. They are rightfully referred to as *horny corals* but this designation may be offensive to some people. The reason they are inexpensive is that they are usually excluded from restrictions and can legally be collected and shipped from most of the Caribbean and South American reefs. They are also small, individual (they don't colonize) and easy to keep alive for a short time if they are not removed from their base which is attached, usually, to a stone.

However, be warned: THEY ARE USUALLY THE MOST DIFFICULT OF ALL SOFT CORALS. They are definitely not for beginners.

The gorgonians require feeding which is easily accomplished by using a food baster to blow newly hatched brine shrimp or brine shrimp mash (made by liquidizing

MELITHAEA SPECIES, THE ORANGE SEA FAN FROM THE RED SEA, REQUIRES BACK LIGHTING AND TOP LIGHTING, FEEDING, MODEST WATER MOVEMENT AND EXPERTISE IN MINI-REEF MANAGEMENT. THEY DO BEST IN A TANK BY THEMSELVES.

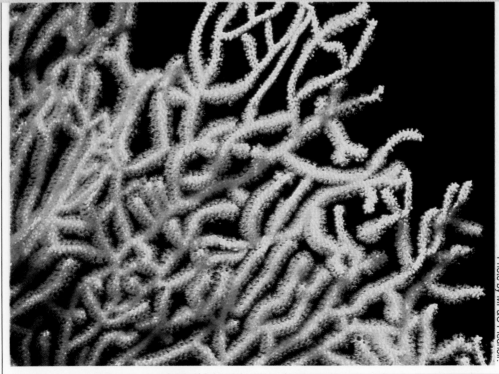

Photo by MP&C Piednoir.

Photo by Walt Deas.

MELITHAEA ACABARIA, THE GOLDEN SEA FAN FROM AUSTRALIA, REQUIRES THE SAME CARE AS ALL MELITHAEA WITH TOP AND BACK LIGHTING. THEY DO BEST IN A TANK BY THEMSELVES.

brine shrimp) across their opened polyps. Their tan colors indicate they are assisted by zooxanthellae (symbiotic algae) for their nutritional needs, thus they need light. But that's part of the problem. These tall, slender corals grow from the bottom of the tank to the top. Obviously they get stronger light the taller they grow. Maybe that's why they are so difficult to maintain.

In general those gorgonians with thick, heavy branches are easier to maintain than gorgonians with thin fingers.

Get advice from your source of purchase as to how they should be maintained because so much has to do with the quality of the water and the intensity of light. They do not require water which is too agitated, but some constant water movement is desirable.

If these flower animals intrigue you, your best bet at success is to maintain them in their own aquarium. Helpful aids are a water flow system which effectively gives a moderate current uniformly over the whole flower animal, a biological filtering system that removes all the harmful nitrogen-bearing chemicals, a protein water skimmer and uniform, low level

Photo by Walt Deas.

MELITHAEA OCHRACEA, THE FRILLED SAN FAN, REQUIRES BACK AND TOP LIGHTING AND TECHNICAL SUPPORT INCLUDING SPECIAL FILTRATION. CERTAINLY NOT RECOMMENDED FOR THE BEGINNER.

lighting uniformly all over the aquarium. One or two white fluorescents at the top of the tank and tubes lighting the back and sides are helpful. They can be turned off during viewing because the back lights are annoying to the viewer.

Care must be taken that there are no filamentous algae. Mini-reefers who are successful at keeping gorgonians have reached the pinnacle of success. If they keep these flower animals they can keep almost anything else.

Like many of the soft corals, the gorgonians shed their skin once or twice weekly. This skin can be deadly to some other corals, that's why we need such a heavy filtration system in gorgonian tanks.

In conclusion: if you are a beginner, forsake gorgonians until you have at least one year of successful experience as a mini-reefer. In all cases start with your gorgonians in a separate tank.

MELITHAEA SPECIES FROM THE RED SEA ARE EASILY REMOVED AND SHIPPED BUT THEY DO NOT THRIVE UNDER ORDINARY MINI-REEF CONDITIONS. PHOTO BY MP&C PIEDNOIR AQUA PRESS.

ACANTHOGORGIA SPECIES ABOVE AND **MELITHAEA** BELOW SPECIES ARE
MAGNIFICENT AND GREATLY ENTICE MINI-REEFERS TO MAINTAIN THEM IN
THEIR HOMES, BUT THEY HAVE SPECIAL REQUIREMENTS WHICH ARE BEST
SERVED IN THEIR OWN, SEPARATE AQUARIUM.

Photos by Walt Deas.

A FEATHER STAR ON AN ORANGE SEA FAN (ABOVE). *SUBERGORGIA MOLLIS*, THE GOLDEN GORGONIA, BELOW, CAN BE SUCCESSFULLY MAINTAINED USING THE DRIP METHOD OF CONSTANTLY ADDING NEW WATER WITH REPLENISHED TRACE ELEMENTS. BUT THEY REQUIRE BACK LIGHTING AS WELL AS TOP LIGHTING AND, ESSENTIALLY, DO BEST IN THEIR OWN MINI-REEF TANK.

Photos by Walt Deas.

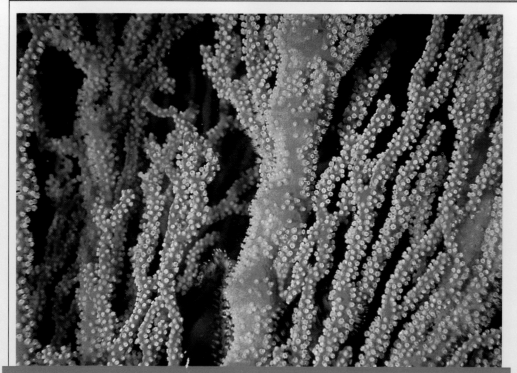

MELITHAEA SPECIES, SIMILAR TO *ACANTHOGORGIA,* HAS BEEN SUCCESSFULLY MAINTAINED IN THE MINI-REEF TANK FOLLOWING THE INSTRUCTIONS FOR SEA FANS. THE PHOTO BELOW SHOWS *MELITHAEA ACABARIA,* THE GOLDEN SEA FAN, IN ITS NOT-SO-GOLDEN PHASE.

Photos by Walt Deas.

A BRITTLE STAR ON A DEEP WATER (200 FEET) *MELITHAEA* SPECIES. THE DEEP WATER SPECIES SEEM TO DO BETTER IN THE MINI-REEF TANK BECAUSE THEY REQUIRE VERY LITTLE LIGHT. THIS GORGONIAN IS SIMPLY CALLED THE DEEP WATER SEA FAN. IN THE PHOTO BELOW, THE RED-VEINED SEA FAN, *MELITHAEA* SPECIES, ALSO SEEMS TO DO WELL IN THE MINI-REEF TANK BUT REQUIRES EXPERT CARE ESPECIALLY AS FAR AS LIGHTING IS CONCERNED.

Photos by Walt Deas.

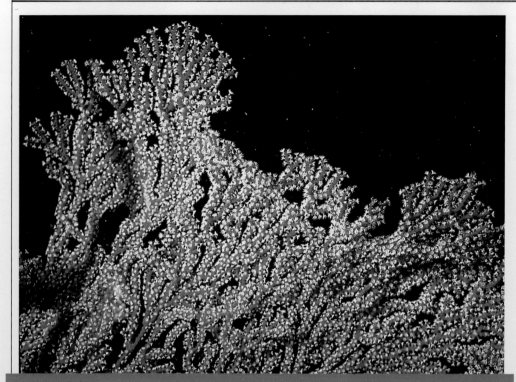

ABOVE IS THE CHRISTMAS SEA FAN, *MELITHAEA* SPECIES. BELOW IS THE YELLOW-SPOTTED SEA FAN, *ACANTHOGORGIA* SPECIES. BOTH ARE DIFFICULT TO CARE FOR AND REQUIRE BACK AND TOP LIGHTING AS WELL AS UNIFORM WATER MOVEMENT. THEY ARE BEST MAINTAINED IN THEIR OWN MINI-REEF AQUARIUM.

Photos by Walt Deas and MP&C Piednoir.

SUBERGORGIA SPECIES ABOVE, THE GOLDEN GORGONIAN AND MELITHAEA ACABARIA, THE GOLDEN SEA FAN IN ITS YELLOW PHASE. BOTH ARE DIFFICULT TO MAINTAIN BUT YOU HAVE A CHANCE IF YOU CAREFULLY FOLLOW THE INSTRUCTIONS IN THE TEXT.

Photos by Walt Deas.

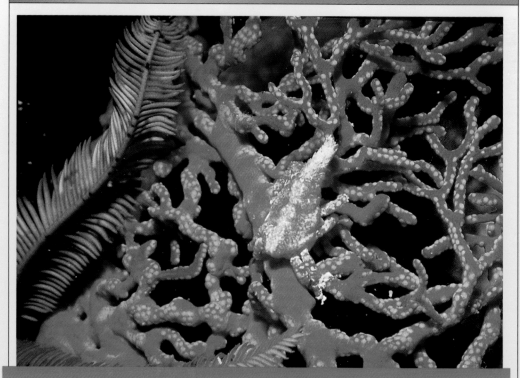

THE GORGONIAN CRAB, *XENOCARCINUS DEPRESSUS* SCAVENGES THE BLUSHING SEA FAN, *MELITHAEA* SPECIES. BELOW A CLOSEUP OF THE MAGENTA SEA FAN, *MELITHAEA* SPECIES.

Photos by Walt Deas.

THIS GIANT SEA FAN IS THE GOLDEN GORGONIAN, *SUBERGORGIA MOLLIS*. IT HAS BEEN SUCCESSFULLY MAINTAINED IN PUBLIC AQUARIUMS WHICH HAVE RUNNING SEA WATER, BUT NO ONE SEEMS TO HAVE TRIED THIS IN THE MINI-REEF AQUARIUM. PHOTO BY WALT DEAS

MELITHAEA SPECIES ARE SO ATTRACTIVE THAT MANY BEGINNERS ARE TEMPTED TO BUY THEM. RESIST THE TEMPTATION. TO GROW A HAMMERED SEA FAN LIKE THIS ONE REQUIRES GREAT SKILL AND LOTS OF LUCK. THE LUCK COMES IN WHEN THE SEA FAN WAS COLLECTED AND HOW MUCH ABUSE IT TOOK. IF THEY ARE CAREFULLY REMOVED FROM THEIR BIRTHPLACE, THEY HAVE A FAIR CHANCE OF SURVIVING IN THE MINI-REEF AQUARIUM PROVIDING THEY GET BACK LIGHTING AS WELL AS TOP LIGHTING AND GENTLE BUT THOROUGH WATER MOVEMENT. PHOTO BY MP&C PIEDNOIR AQUA PRESS.

AN UNKNOWN TRANSPARENT GOBY ON THIS *SUBERGORGIA* SPECIES. THE GOBIES AND OTHER LIVING THINGS SEEM TO KEEP THE SEA FANS CLEAN. PHOTO BY WALT DEAS.

A DIVER WITH A DEEP WATER *MELITHAEA* SPECIES. THE DEEP WATER SEA FANS HAVE THE GREATEST CHANCE OF SURVIVAL IN THE HOME MINI-REEF AQUARIUM.

CORAL ANEMONES, FALSE CORALS, MUSHROOM ANEMONES, DISK ANEMONES

THE BROWN MUSHROOM CORAL, *ACTINODISCUS* SPECIES, IS EASILY MAINTAINED IN THE AQUARIUM WITH 5 HOURS OF INTENSE LIGHTING PER DAY, SLOW WATER MOVEMENTS AND ISOLATION FROM OTHER FLOWER ANIMALS.

Photo by Dr. Herbert R. Axelrod.

THE ORDER CORALLIMORPHARIA
Stephenson, 1937

We can add another hundred or more flower animals to our mini-reef catalogue by suggesting that corallimorphs be considered because they are so easy to care for. They need normal light, say three white fluorescent tubes for 8 hours a day. They only need normal water movement from an ordinary water pump. If there is too much light or too much water current they signal you immediately by closing up, or at least by not expanding completely.

The order is split into two families, the Corallimorphidae and the Actinodiscidae. Identification of these flower animals as to their genus and species is not easy for the beginner. Use the photos as a guide and experiment with their care. These animals are adaptable and even beginners enjoy successes with maintenance and breeding them in their normal mini-reef aquariums.

The *Actinodiscis* and the *Rhodactis* species reap most of their nutritional needs from their symbiotic algae, thus they need

THE GREEN-RINGED ANEMONE CORAL, *ACTINODISCUS* SPECIES, IS EASILY MAINTAINED IN THE MINI-REEF AQUARIUM WITH 5 HOURS OF INTENSE LIGHTING, SLOW-MOVING WATERS AND ISOLATION. THESE CAN BE PLANTED ON THE BOTTOM OF THE TANK WHERE THE LIGHT IS LOWEST AND THE WATER IS MOST PLACID.

Photo by U. Erich Friese.

THE BROWN GIANT CUP, *AMPLEXIDISCUS* SPECIES, IS RELATIVELY SAFE IN THE MINI-REEF AQUARIUM WITH 5 HOURS OF LIGHT, SLOW WATER MOVEMENT AND ROOM TO EXPAND.

slightly stronger light than those flower animals which aren't blessed with these algae. I have been able to keep these species for six months without feeding them, but I always had a few harmless fishes in the mini-reef with them. But for them to grow, reproduce and really be in the best of condition, they require feedings of brine shrimp if they have tentacles which can trap them. For those flower animals without tentacles, they have to absorb their nutrition through their entire structure.

The *Discosoma* are interesting feeders. They normally occur with their disks in the horizontal position. When food animals are sensed, they form a circular, hollow cup in which they can even trap fishes, crabs and snails.

Reproduction of the *Actinodiscus* in the aquarium is simple. The flower animals do it all by themselves. They form adjacent animals which are not physically connected to their neighbors. This is done by splitting. Since these flower animals can move (but very slowly), the mother *Actinodiscus* leaves her offspring once it becomes established. All of this occurs without the assistance of the mini-reefer, but it is interesting to observe and recognize. Once the mother disk animal has moved a short distance away, it re-attaches itself to the substrata and prepares for further spawning.

Rhodactis spawn in a similar manner but they split lengthwise after their mouth elongates and divides. The rest of the animal then divides along this pattern. The mother animals of this genus do not move away, instead they sort of colonize and become a tangled mass.

The control of the water chemistry is very helpful in keeping all coral animals alive and healthy. As with freshwater aquariums, the most destructive buildup results from over feeding. No only does the uneaten food rot and produce nitrates and phosphates, but the feces of over-fed fishes contains undigested food particles which are equally as bad as the uneaten food particles. Therefore filters with denitrification capacities are highly recommended.

Keeping a satisfactory mini-reef aquarium is not an inexpensive hobby. Don't start with a mini-reef aquarium unless you are willing and able to support it financially. Start out with sufficient quality lights, pumps, filters and space (large tanks) to give yourself the proper chance to be successful.

AMPLEXIDISCUS SPECIES, THE GOLDEN GIANT MUSHROOM CORAL, EATING A MUSSEL!

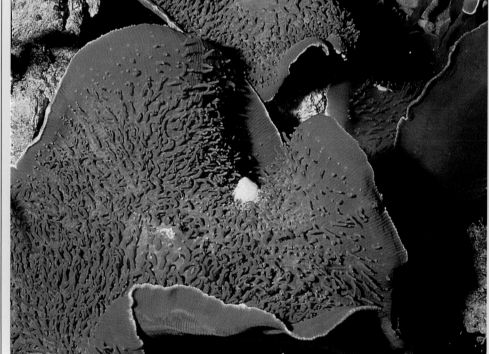

Photo by MP&C Piednoir Aqua Press.

THE SAME *AMPLEXIDISCUS* SPECIES, THE GOLDEN GIANT MUSHROOM CORAL, SWALLOWING THE MUSSEL BY CLOSING ITSELF OVER THE SHELLFISH.

TWO *ACTINODISCUS* SPECIES. THE BLUE GIANT MUSHROOM SHOWN ABOVE HAS A SMOOTH SURFACE WHILE THE PIMPLED BROWN MUSHROOM, *ACTINODISCUS* SPECIES SHOWN BELOW, HAS PIMPLES.

Photos by U.Erich Friese.

Photo by U. Erich Friese.

ABOVE: *ACTINODISCUS* SPECIES EXPANDED, A SIGHT YOU DON'T OFTEN SEE. THE COMMON NAME IS THE GIANT GREEN MUSHROOM. IT IS EASILY CARED FOR IN THE MINI-REEF TANK. BELOW: THE FALSE CORAL, *RHODACTIS* SPECIES.

Photo by R. Wederich.

THE BROWN MUSHROOM, *ACTINODISCUS* SPECIES, IS EASILY MAINTAINED IN THE AQUARIUM WITH 5 HOURS OF INTENSE LIGHTING AND SLOW WATER MOVEMENTS. KEEP IT FROM TOUCHING OTHER FLOWER ANIMALS.

Photo by U. Erich Friese.

ACTINODISCUS SPECIES ARE WONDERFUL IN THE MINI-REEF TANK. THEY HAVE A WIDE RANGE OF LIGHT TOLERANCES SO THEY CAN BE PLANTED AT DIFFERENT LEVELS IN THE TANK (=DIFFERENT QUANTITY AND QUALITY OF LIGHT ENERGY). THEY DO BEST LOW IN THE TANK WHERE THE WATER IS NOT TOO ACTIVE.

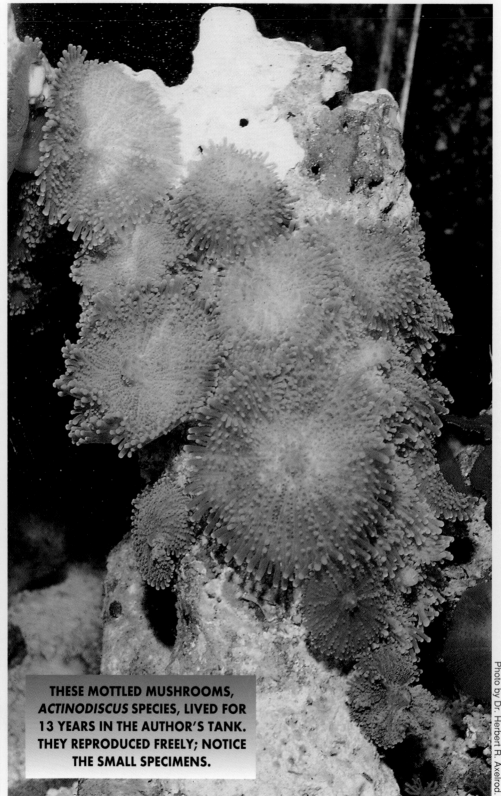

THESE MOTTLED MUSHROOMS, *ACTINODISCUS* SPECIES, LIVED FOR 13 YEARS IN THE AUTHOR'S TANK. THEY REPRODUCED FREELY; NOTICE THE SMALL SPECIMENS.

Photo by Dr. Herbert R. Axelrod.

ACTINODISCUS COERULEUS, THE BLUE MUSHROOM CORAL, IS ATTRACTIVE AND EASILY CARED FOR IN THE MINI-REEF TANK.

Photo by MP&C Piednoir Aqua Press.

THESE TWO *ACTINODISCUS* SPECIES REQUIRE THE SAME TREATMENT. THEY THRIVE WITH MINIMAL LIGHT AND SLOW WATER MOTION. THEY ARE CALLED MANY THINGS IN THE AQUARIUM WORLD SUCH AS CORAL ANEMONES, FALSE CORALS, MUSHROOM ANEMONES AND DISK ANEMONES. IF YOU CALL THEM MUSHROOMS YOUR DEALER WILL KNOW WHAT YOU MEAN. PHOTO BY DR. HERBERT R. AXELROD.

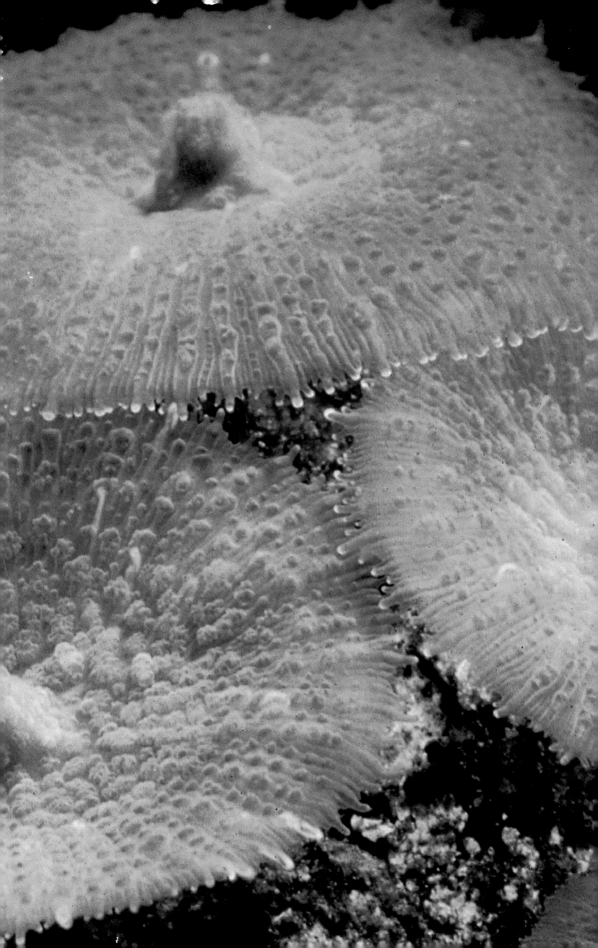

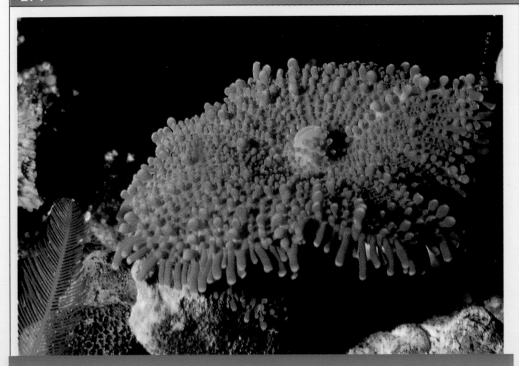

THE COMMON MUSHROOM CORAL, *ACTINODISCUS* SPECIES, IS A WELCOME
ADDITION TO EVERY MINI-REEF TANK. YOU DON'T SEE MANY MINI-REEFERS
THAT DON'T INCLUDE THIS GENUS IN THEIR COLLECTION.

Photo by MP&C Piednoir

CORAL CARE

Maintaining your living corals in your mini-reef tank is as much an art as a science. No hobbyist can be expected to monitor continuously such physical parameters as temperature, salinity, chemical pollutants (ammonia, nitrogen compounds, etc.), pH, clarity, biological contents (micro-algae, microscopic living organisms) and other factors which contribute to the well-being of a mini-reef. Of course many of

Pet shops carry a full range of canister filters which can successfully manage the water movement, filtration and, in some cases, the temperature in your mini-reef aquarium. Photo courtesy of Eheim.

these variables can be measured INTERMITTENTLY and, as a mini-reefer, you are expected to have the necessary equipment with which to conduct these measurements and to compare them to acceptable standards. You also have to be able to do something about problems.

If your mini-reef is too cold, then you need more heat. This may mean another heater, a larger heater, insulation of the bottom, back and sides of the aquarium, a relocation, or whatever...BUT YOU MUST BE PREPARED TO DO SOMETHING. This problem is only if the tank is too cold. What if the tank is too warm???

Many mini-reef problems are as complex as is this seemingly simple temperature parameter.

We can do something to handle almost all of these problems by supplying remedies continuously. I don't mean *medicines* when I say *remedies*. I mean remedying deteriorating situations before they become incurable. The techniques which have proven successful deal with HEATING, AERATION, FILTRATION, LIGHTING and CHEMICAL SUPPLEMENTS.

FILTRATION/AERATION/HEATING

Filtration, heating and aeration are lumped together because you are advised to get a single unit which does it all. There are successful units which do any one or two of these functions. But it is possible to get a unit which does it all. At the present time the *Eheim Professionel Filter* can handle, aeration, various types of filtration, water heating and water movement or current. These are absolutely necessary for the health of your mini-reef aquarium. Ask your local aquarium shop to help you select the model best suited for your needs. One unit was designed for a 92-gallon aquarium (100-gallon aquariums usually contain 92-gallons of water); the other for a 158-gallon aquarium. For larger tanks you can use more than one unit. I prefer using multiple smaller units in case of a breakdown or where corals require separate water movements. They have wet/dry versions which utilize bacterial colonization to break down the nitrites and ammonia. The Eheims move a lot of water. Their model 2229, for example, pushes almost 300 gallons per hour!

LIGHTING

Many corals contain zooxanthellae, the symbiotic algae. These brown algae require light. Various corals require more or less light in terms of time and intensity. Obviously leather corals and corals which do not require strong lighting should be placed farther away from the light source than corals requiring strong

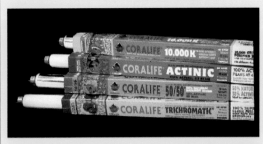

Pet shops carry lamps in both standard output and VHO (very high output) to insure that your corals receive the quantity and quality of light they need to survive. Photo courtesy of Energy Savers.

lighting. In theory corals which do not REQUIRE strong lighting can still thrive in a strongly lit situation, BUT the danger of over-lighting is the uncontrolled growth of algae. Most thread algae can be killers of corals.

Lights for the coral mini-reef can be fluorescent lamps mounted on the cover in a reflector; some metal halide lights which can be located a few feet from the tank because

being closer generates too much heat within the mini-reef aquarium. Metal halides are great if you have the room because they are powerful, produce a full color spectrum and are excellent point sources of light for corals which have special light requirements. Of course you can have both fluorescent and metal halide lighting, probably using them at different times.

Fluorescent lamps are available in different lengths (18", 24", 36" and 48") and in two basic outputs, standard output and VHO (*very high output*). Trichromatic lights, made by Coralife, provide a high intensity, full-spectrum daylight similar to what the sun puts out in the unpolluted air of the tropics. They even have actinic lamps and 50/50 lamps which are half actinic and half trichromatic. These are all fluorescent tubes which start losing power after their first day of operation. They are usually only of value when they have less than 2,500 hours of use. If you can get an electric timer which keeps a running total of the time your lights are on (tanning studios use these timers for their machines), it would be helpful. I use my camera light meter. I set the light meter when the lamps are new. At an ASA rating of 100, my lens setting should be f/32. When the light meter rating drops so that I now need f/16, it is time to change the lamps. Or, if you want to run your lamps for 8 hours per day, you know you have about 300 days of life in the lamps. That's ten months, so just mark your calendar!

Corals may suffer trace element deficiency. It is absolutely necessary for most coral animals to have such trace elements as iodine, strontium and calcium in order to thrive. Pet shops offer these products for mini-reefers. Photo courtesy of Boyd Enterprises.

CHEMICAL SUPPLEMENTS

Corals and other animals in the mini-reef aquarium depend on trace elements dissolved in the water in which they live. You must start your mini-reef tank with the best salts available. These salts MUST contain trace elements...necessary trace elements. By far the most important trace elements are strontium and calcium for the hard corals and iodine compounds for the soft corals. Your local aquarium shop should have stocks of various additives with instructions on how to use them.

In general, the use of lights, filters, aerators (= water movements and directions of currents) and chemical supplements depends upon your experience. When corals begin to fail they may have a shortfall in one of these categories. They may also be fatally wounded during shipment or suffer a disease. Recognizing a failing coral flower

animal requires experience. That's the ART part of maintaining a mini-reef. There is simply no substitute for experience. If you want the best experience, spend as much time as possible in your local aquarium shop and compare qualities of corals. Inquire why a particular coral looks different from specimen to specimen. Join an aquarium society. Do everything possible to gain experience and then share your experiences with others by submitting articles and photographs to TROPICAL FISH HOBBYIST MAGAZINE.

Don't even attempt to maintain corals in your mini-reef aquarium without getting the best possible salt which is enhanced with trace elements and made especially for aquarium purposes. Artificial sea salts are widely available in a number of different formulations. This has made the keeping of corals and mini-reef aquariums possible for hobbyists living thousands of miles away from natural seawater sources. Photo courtesy of Coralife/Energy Savers

GLOSSARY

Courtesy of Dr. Elizabeth M. Wood

Ahermatypic: corals that lack zooxanthellae and do not contribute to reef-building.

Atoll: a roughly circular reef that encloses a central lagoon.

Axial: referring to the corallite formed at the tip of a branch.

Back reef: a shallow, usually impoverished, part of the reef facing away from the reef front toward land or shallow water.

Bank reef: a reef formed by growth of corals on an underwater hillock. The top of the reef is not exposed.

Barrier reef: a reef formed at the margin between the continental shelf and deep oceanic waters.

Biotope: an area with particular physical and biological features; *e.g.,* reef front, lagoon, back reef, exposed fore reef, etc.

Calice: upper, open end of the corallite.

Cerioid: closely packed corallites with fused walls.

Coenosarc: an extension of the polyp that stretches over the surface of the skeleton.

Coenosteum: skeletal material deposited outside the corallite wall.

Colline: elongate wall or ridge formed between corallites or groups of corallites.

Columella: a skeletal structure that develops in the central axis of the calice. It is usually either styliform (rod-like), papillose, trabecular (both spongy in appearance) or lamellar (formed from a series of interconnecting vertical plates).

Corallite: skeletal parts deposited by a single polyp.

Corallum: the skeleton of solitary and colonial corals.

Costae: extension of the septa outside the corallite wall.

Dendroid: corallum formed from spreading branches of single corallites.

Dissepiments: skeletal structures left by the polyps.

Ecomorph: an intraspecific variant produced in response to environmental factors.

Edge zone: a horizontal fold of the polyp wall that extends over the corallite wall.

Etymology: formation and meaning of words.

Explanate: spread out flat.

Exsert: a term used to describe septa that protrude above the top of the corallite wall.

Extratentacular (=intercalicular): describing a form of asexual reproduction in corals in which a new mouth is produced from the edge zone or coenosarc and thus lies outside the parental ring of tentacles.

Flabellate: corallum in which the meanders arise from a common base but are free laterally. They may be relatively short (crescentic) or elongate and sinuous (flabello-meandroid).

Fore reef: the main seaward facing part of the reef, stretching from shallow to deep water.

Fossa: the central depression in a calice, usually partly filled by the columella.

Fringing reef: reef growing adjacent to island or mainland shores.

Hermatypic: corals that contain zooxanthellae and contribute to the building of reefs.

Hydrocorals: hydrozoan coelenterates that produce a calcareous skeleton.

Imperforate: referring to skeletal structures in corals *(e.g.,* walls, septa, coenosteum) that are solid rather than porous.

Insert: a term used to describe septa which do not protrude above the top of the corallite wall.

Intratentacular (=intracalicular): describing a form of asexual reproduction in corals in which the oral disc invaginates to produce a new mouth within the parental ring of tentacles.

Isotherm: a line linking points of equal temperature.

Meandroid: corallum in which the corallites are fused in longitudinal series to produce a pattern of valleys and ridges.

Mesenteries/mesenterial filaments: the mesenteries are radial partitions lying within the gastrovascular cavity of the coral polyp; mesenterial filaments may be produced from their free inner margins.

Oceanic reef: a reef that has its base in deep oceanic waters.

Octocorals: alcyonarian coelenterates that produce a calcareous skeleton.

Oral disc: upper surface of the polyp, extending from the mouth to the outer ring of tentacles.

Paliform lobe: a vertical lobe-like protrusion formed at the inner end of a septum, adjacent to the columella.

Perforate: referring to skeletal structures in corals (e.g., walls, septa, coenosteum) that are porous rather than solid.

Peristome: area within the inner ring of tentacles and immediately surrounding the mouth.

Peritheca: surface of the coenosteum between the corallites.

Phaceloid: growth form in which tall, separate corallites arise from the basal part of the corallum.

Planula: the planktonic larval stage of corals.

Platform reef: a reef formed by growth of corals on an underwater hillock.

Plocoid: separate, well defined corallites.

Polymorphic: existing in more than one form.

Polyp: the living part of a coral.

Reef crest: an emergent part of the reef, just behind the reef front.

Scleractinian: true or stony corals belonging to the Class Zoantharia.

Septa: calcareous, plate-like structures that radiate from the wall toward the center of the corallite. They are aligned vertically and alternate with the mesenteries.

Septal cycles: relating to the formation and arrangement of the septa. Septa are laid down in radial series or cycles, the first cycle consisting of six primary septa, the second of six secondary septa, the third of 12 tertiary septa, and so on.

Septal margin: the upper free edge of the septum.

Septal orders: relating to the size of septa. Equal sized septa form a single order; subequal or unequal septa form two or more orders. Orders do not necessarily correspond to cycles (see above).

Septocostae: extensions of the septa that unite adjacent calice centers. They are found in corals where the corallites lack walls and there is no clear distinction between septa and costae.

Shelf reef: a reef that has its base on the relatively shallow floor of the continental shelf.

Solitary: referring to corals that grow as a single polyp with a surrounding skeleton.

Synapticulae: small bars that make lateral links between adjacent septa.

Thamnasterioid: a corallum in which corallite walls are indistinct and the septa run uninterrupted between calice centers.

Trochoid: top shaped.

Turbinate: shaped like an inverted cone.

Zooxanthellae: unicellular algae (dinoflagellates) that live in coral tissues.

INDEX

Page numbers in **boldface** refer to illustrations.

BIBLIOGRAPHY

BOOKS THAT YOU SHOULD READ TO BETTER UNDERSTAND KEEPING LIVING CORALS IN YOUR MINI-REEF AQUARIUM. These books are available from your local pet shop. The prices listed here are SUGGESTED retail prices and the prices may vary from one area to another. It is cheaper to buy these books from your local pet shop as they do not charge for postage and handling.

CORALS OF THE WORLD
Dr. Elizabeth M. Wood

This book is recognized world-wide as the most authoritative book on the classification of corals. There are color photos of each genus plus monochrome photos of the skeleton to make identification simpler. The book has 290 wonderful photos. 260 pages, 8.5 x 11", heavy coated paper, sewn and hard bound.

Suggested retail $79.95 ISBN 0-86622-657-5

MARINE INVERTEBRATES AND PLANTS OF THE LIVING REEF
Dr. Patrick Colin

This is THE handbook for mini-reefers as it discusses and illustrates all THE ANIMALS SUITABLE FOR MAINTENANCE IN THE MINI-REEF (except fishes). Though it is limited to the Caribbean, these same animals (or animals like them) are found throughout the tropical seas and the information contained in this book applies to all mini-reef invertebrates including the Pacific species as well. 512 pages, 5.5 x 8.5", 600 color photos, hard cover, sewn.

Suggested retail price $39.95. ISBN 0-87666-460-5

MARINE FISHES AND INVERTEBRATES IN YOUR OWN HOME
Dr. Cliff W. Emmens

Prof. Dr. Emmens is the dean of mini-reefers. He has maintained a mini-reef exhibit in his home since 1963. This is a very authoritative book as well as a beautiful book with magnificent color photos. It only deals with mini-reef animals. Hard cover, 192 pages, 8.5 x 11", sewn for permanence, 315 color photos.

Suggested retail price $39.95. ISBN 0-86622-790-3

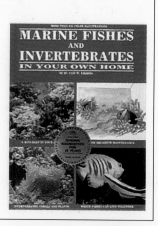

THE ENCYCLOPEDIA OF MARINE INVERTEBRATES
by Panel of Expert Mini-reefers

This book covers EVERY invertebrate group of interest to mini-reefers and marine aquarists. It is a huge book of 736 pages, 5.5 x 8.5 with more than 600 color photographs most of which appear nowhere else. Sewn and hard bound.

Suggested retail is $89.95. ISBN 0-86622-141-7

SEA ANEMONES AS A HOBBY
U.Erich Friese

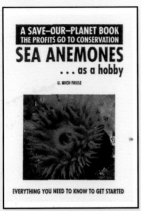

Sea anemones have a very important place in the mini-reef both as a refuge for certain fishes and to purify the tank as they snare and eat small infusorians which cloud and foul the water. This colorful and interesting books advises you in the care and selection of sea anemones for your mini-reef aquarium. If you don't have sea anemones in your mini-reef then you really don't have a mini-reef aquarium.

Suggested retail price is $49.95. Hard cover, sewn. 320 pages size 7 x 10" with more than 150 unique color photographs. ISBN 0-86622-539-0

MARINE INVERTEBRATES
U. Erich Friese

Written by the chief aquarist at the aquarium in Sydney, Australia, this book is loaded with tips on water chemistry, how reef animals get along with each other, and how to keep and breed most of the animals mini-reefers keep in their home aquariums. Friese probably has more experience with more mini-reefers than any non-professional aquarist. 240 pages size 5 x 8", 120 color photos, hard bound.

Suggested retail price $29.95. ISBN 0-86622-708-3

THE SUCCESSFUL MINI-REEF AQUARIUM
U. Erich Friese

This book provides all of the information anyone will need to set up a mini-reef aquarium and keep its rich diversity of marine life going in good health. Fully illustrated throughout with full-color photos, the book leads readers step by easy-to-understand step through all of the practical considerations involved. 320 pages, size 7x10", 200 full-color photos, hard bound.

Suggested retail price $47.95. ISBN 0-7938-2093-6

These books can be ordered from your local pet shop. If you order from TFH, please add $4.50 per book for postage.

T.F.H.PUBLICATIONS, INC., 1 TFH PLAZA, NEPTUNE CITY, N.J. 0775